Decision Analysis:
An Overview

Decision Analysis: An Overview

Rex V. Brown

Decisions and Designs, Inc.
Formerly Associate Professor of Business Administration
University of Michigan

Andrew S. Kahr

Cameron Peterson

Decisions and Designs, Inc.
Associate Professor of Psychology
University of Michigan

Holt, Rinehart and Winston

New York   Chicago   San Francisco   Atlanta   Dallas
Montreal   Toronto   London   Sydney

Library of Congress Cataloging in Publication Data

Brown, Rex. V.
Decision analysis: an overview.

(Series in quantitative methods for decision making)
Includes bibliographical references.
1. Decision-making. I. Kahr, Andrew S., joint author.
II. Peterson, Cameron, joint author.   III. Title
HD69.D4B76   658.4'03   74-1212

ISBN: 0-03-088408-X

Printed in the United States of America
6 7 8 9   090   9 8 7 6 5 4

Dedicated to Robert Schlaifer,
pioneer and inspiration
in the development of decision analysis
for the business manager.

PREFACE

Decision analysis is a discipline for systematic evaluation of alternative actions as a basis for choice among them. Decision makers in business, industry, government, and other organizations are currently applying this discipline to their everday problems and policy formation. Such application involves setting up models of the problems to be analyzed, selecting inputs to the models that quantify the judgments of those responsible for the decisions, and deriving the models' outputs from these inputs. Decision analysis models are highly flexible. They can be as simple as routine cash-flow projections or so complex as to require the use of a computer. However, a fundamental body of concepts and techniques underlies all these specifics. This book provides an overview of these fundamentals—not in the abstract but in use.

Decision analysis models often include a decision tree or decision diagram. Inputs to such models can include numerical probabilities, that quantify judgments about uncertain future events, as well as numerical assessments that express the decision maker's attitudes, or the organization's policies, as regards the assumption of risk. A model's outputs may include a display of the probabilities of each possible outcome for every action alternative, or a specification of the single course of action to be preferred under the assumptions of the model.

One of the characteristics distinguishing decision analysis from other quantitative tools available to managers is that these other techniques—such as operations research, Bayesian statistics, mathematical programming—embrace much more narrowly applicable classes of models. Specific operations research models, for example, may be useful in selecting warehouse sites, in balancing assembly-line facilities, or in forecasting sales growth; but none of these models will fit the great majority of the large and small decisions faced by managers who must plan and implement business strategies. Decision analysis, on the contrary, can usefully address any problem meriting more than momentary consideration.

It is largely for this reason that decision analysis, which entered professional management training and practice during the early 1960s, has enjoyed a rapidly growing role in a wide range of industries and problem settings. Applications have ranged from decisions regarding product development to production facility, pricing, and other marketing and financial problems. The discipline has been uniquely helpful in resolving choices between actions with complex and uncertain future effects—effects that, in themselves, frequently depend in part on subsequent decisions. However, as a systematic approach to making choices, it has contributed valuable insights in many situations that initially seemed barely complicated or substantial enough to merit writing any numbers down on paper at all.

Chapter 5 of this book explores in greater depth the experience of major companies in applying decision analysis to their operations. The preceding chapters, the heart of the book, present a detailed case study of a decision analysis application, the Ore case. This case is in the form of a dialogue between a manager, who is assumed to have had no prior exposure to the field, and a specialist consultant. The case shows how decision analysis proceeds from simple to more complex models. More importantly, it shows how the logic and outputs of such an analysis can be made comprehensible and persuasive to an operating manager who had had no previous training.

The exercises in the book have been designed to help the reader extend and test his understanding and begin to apply decision analysis to his own problems. The book is suitable for independent reading and study by the manager or student, or it can serve as text for an eight-to-ten class segment in an advanced undergraduate or masters level course—either a quantitative-methods course or one directed to a specific functional field where decision analysis has fruitful application, such as the fields of marketing, production, and finance.

Using the book in any of these ways, the reader can expect to gain an appreciation of how, where, and why decision analysis works, and a sensitivity to the conditions of setting and application under which it can be employed most effectively. The book, short as it is, should have a perceptible impact on the manager's confidence and effectiveness in decision making. However, it cannot teach him all that he might usefully know about the field, nor can it substitute for the benefits of actual application experience. To make insightful, consistent application over a range of important problems, he will want to have the benefit either of further training, or of consulting or other specialized assistance.

The authors' longer book, *Decision Analysis for the Manager* (New York: Holt, Rinehart and Winston, 1974), is aimed at providing the additional techniques and practice needed to equip the manager to make broad, competent application of decision analysis, not only to enhance his individual capability, but also to upgrade the quality of management decision making in the organization as a whole.

January, 1974

R. Brown

A. Kahr

C. Peterson

ABOUT THE AUTHORS

All three authors are currently applying decision analysis techniques for clients in the public and private sectors. All three were previously on university faculties developing and teaching these techniques—Dr. Kahr at the Harvard Business School, Dr. Peterson at the University of Michigan, and Dr. Brown at both. In addition, Dr. Kahr has been Vice President of Finance at Ventron Corporation.

CONTENTS

Decision Analysis:
An Overview

INTRODUCTION

Almost everyone makes a great many decisions every day, usually without the aid of any numbers or even of pencil and paper. We decide what to eat for lunch, what route to follow in driving to school or office, what television program to watch, and—less frequently—some weightier matters also. This book is directed to managers and to students of management and thus is primarily concerned with the kinds of decisions that are made within and on behalf of business enterprises and similar organizations. These *business decisions* are like the familiar personal decisions of daily life in one very significant respect—the vast majority of business decisions, like the bulk of purely personal decisions, must be and are made on the basis of very little data, figure work, and thought. The busy executive cannot afford the time for prolonged deliberation as to what letters he will write Monday morning (or even as to what he will say in most of them) any more than in his non-business life can he afford to ponder over his choice of breakfast cereal.

A relatively few business decisions (but still a great many every week in a company of even moderate size) are of sufficient importance to merit more extensive and perhaps more formal consideration. In such cases the executive is apt to obtain and write down some figures pertaining to the matter, perform some calculations or analysis, and put together a report, recommendation, or other document intended to justify the selection of one course of action in preference to others. The amount of time and effort needed to prepare and present his analysis and conclusions will depend mainly on how much is at stake in the decision (as the executive sees it) and on how difficult it is to see and prove which course of action is the "right" one.

In principle it can be argued that time and effort should be invested in decision making, as in any other corporate activity, to the extent that this investment will yield a higher return than investment of the same resources in other activities. A sales manager must decide how many hours to spend in his office analyzing pricing and advertising decisions rather than on the road calling on customers without knowing for sure how much money he would make for the company doing either. Hours spent analyzing decisions are well spent if they lead to decisions that generate greater profit than would have been earned if these hours had been otherwise invested.

We are convinced that modern methods of decision making, such as those to be presented in this book, could make sizable contributions to the efficiency and financial success of most businesses. However, it does not follow that managers should necessarily spend more time or more money analyzing and making decisions and less time "running the business." (A rough rule of thumb, suggested by Ronald A. Howard of Stanford University, is that 1 percent of the resources at stake in a decision should be devoted to analyzing that decision.) It is important to employ methods for arriving at better decisions in which managers will justifiably have greater confidence without increasing the amount of time that they must commit to analysis and deliberation. To do this, we must select from a basic kit of tools to deal appropriately with any decision from a small routine problem to an issue of major strategy that places the future of the business at stake.

1.1   GOOD DECISIONS

Unsatisfactory outcomes cannot necessarily be traced to bad decision making. A good bridge player (that is, a good decision maker) may lose to a poor one because of how the cards happened to fall in a particular hand. In the long run, however, we would expect the good player to win. Similarly, an unexpected market development may make a manager sorry he launched a new product even though the decision to do so may have been perfectly sound in terms of the information available at the time. Since good decisions can lead to bad outcomes (and vice versa), decision makers cannot infallibly be graded by their results. Nevertheless, long-term results often provide the best evidence available as to the quality of a man's decisions.

The difference between good and bad *decisions* (as opposed to good and bad *outcomes*) lies partly in the selection of appropriate basic inputs, for example, the discovery of innovative decision options. About this factor we will have little to say. Good decisions require logical handling of these basic inputs, and it is to this process of analysis that our methods are primarily addressed. The best decision cannot be made unless the best option is among those that are being considered. In its most straightforward form decision analysis serves only the function of choosing between options that have already been identified, though not infrequently an attempt at decision analysis in fact suggests new options that had not been thought of before.

1.2 DECISION ANALYSIS AS A NEW TECHNOLOGY

The ability to make sound decisions in the face of inconclusive evidence and unclear personal judgments has always been an enviable skill in business executives and other practical men of affairs. Until recently it was a skill almost entirely in the province of intuition. During World War II formal approaches to decision making began to be introduced under the name of operations research. They were typically applied to special types of clear-cut, repetitive problems, such as those of production control and resource allocation.

Since the 1960s, however, a more general technology has emerged for imposing logical structure on the reasoning that underlies *any* specific decision. This technology is *decision analysis*. Since the mid-1960s there has been a dramatic burgeoning of efforts by major business corporations to adapt this technology to their day-to-day decision making, especially at the most senior level, for example, for acquisitions and new product launchings. Many have found it a way to make better, more defensible, or just less painful decisions. In spite of many obstacles, largely human, which often impede effective implementation, it has been plausibly argued that decision analysis will be to the manager of tomorrow what the slide rule is to the engineer of today.

Decision analysis is a technology that assists individuals and organizations to make up their minds, by quantifying the considerations, however subjective, which enter into any decision. A complex decision problem is decomposed into separable components, often in the form of a decision tree, on which any given decision maker's perception of options, uncertainties, and values can be explicitly represented. Those perceptions are quantified and their logical action implications are deduced according to established technical procedures.

Decision analysis accommodates the same types of considerations as informal decision making; however, it imposes logical structure and discipline on the reasoning. The potential value of decision analysis to an organization's decision making processes is not only in helping individual decision makers to structure their own information and thinking, but also in providing a vehicle for communication between individuals in organizations (for example, in command structures or committees). It may, for example, make it easier to communicate the grounds for a recommendation or identify the areas of potential disagreement. It may also help to focus different types of expertise on different parts of the problem or isolate areas of disagreement between individuals whose recommendations differ.

Actual and potential applications of decision analysis are not restricted to business decisions. They can apply to medical, military, engineering, and governmental decisions as well. Possibly the most ambitious application yet reported specifies under what circumstances the President should order nuclear retaliation.

In the next four chapters of this book we provide a broad overview of the scope, mechanics, and application of decision analysis as a preliminary to building usable skills to enable the reader to analyze his own decisions.

ASSIGNMENTS

1. In your opinion what are the most important qualities distinguishing successful from unsuccessful managers? Where do you put decision-making skills on this list? Which of the qualities that you have listed can be enhanced by formal education, for example, at a business school? Which do you think you have to be born with; which can only be picked up on the job?

2. What is a good decision? Cite a good decision that turned out badly. Give examples of good and bad public decisions, such as by presidents or educational or other institutions?

3. Imagine you are unmarried and "uncommitted." Your best friend phones you to say his (or her) cousin has arrived in town and is free for the evening. Are you interested in a blind date? You are free but want time to make up your mind, so you reply you will call in an hour. All you have been able to find out is that the cousin is your age, is "not bad looking," and has flaming red hair.

    The object of this exercise is to alert you to some considerations that go into making decisions in general. What is your decision? Summarize your reasoning in one paragraph.

4. Discuss the following excerpt from an article by J. Paul Getty, commenting on Getty's view of the role of science in management.

    When I first started drilling in the Oklahoma oil fields, the consensus of expert judgment held that there could be no oil in the so-called Red Beds region. The known "facts" and all specialist opinion would have convinced anyone using conventional scientific method to avoid the Red Beds area. Certainly, if a computer had been available and all the existing data fed into it, the machine would have given a loud and one-sided no.

    But like so many oilmen, I chose to temper all "analytical" thinking with a healthy dose of nonlogical subjectivity. To me the area looked as if it might hide oil. Largely on the basis of a hunch, I decided to see for myself. I began drilling in the Red Beds, struck oil, and brought in a vast new producing field. I rather suspect that by relying on such nontextbook thought processes, and taking attendant risks, the biggest fortunes have been made—in oil and in other endeavors.

Then, too, the business world would be a melancholy one if all decision making were reduced to mathematical equations. If all the risk—and by that I mean not only the dangers, but the zest and the excitement—were removed from business, then the businessman might as well take a civil service job.[1]

[1] J. Paul Getty, "The Fine Art of Being the Boss," *Playboy* (June 1972).

2

THE ORE CASE:
STRUCTURE, PROBABILITY,
AND EXPECTED VALUE

The next three chapters present the ore case as an illustration of how decision analysis can be used to select alternative courses of action. An important goal of this case is to help the reader develop some appreciation of the technical concepts of decision analysis, such as probability, value, utility, and expected value. However, this hypothetical case should be read with the intention of understanding the substantive factors that contribute to the decision in the ore case rather than be read to gain a thorough understanding of the concepts of decision theory. Put yourself in the position of the broker rather than in the position of the decision analyst, and try to figure out what the broker's decision should be. In short, you can best understand decision analysis from the point of view of the manager if you focus on the manager's problem and treat decision theory merely as an aid in solving that problem.

A New York metals broker has just acquired an option to buy 100,000 tons of iron.ore from a Far Eastern government for $5 per ton, which is well below the current world market price of ore. Since other brokers have received the same option, the broker feels that a decision must be made immediately. He is quite certain that he can get about $8 per ton for the ore if he is able to import it, but there is a catch. The United States government may refuse to grant an import license. If this happens, the contract will be annulled and a penalty of $1 per ton imposed.

The $300,000 would be a handsome profit for the broker's firm if the broker goes ahead with the deal and the government agrees to grant an import license. However, the $100,000 loss suffered in case the contract is annulled constitutes a serious one. Consequently, the broker decides to call in a decision analyst to help him make the decision.

What follows in Chapters 2, 3, and 4 is a dialogue that transpired upon the arrival of the broker's analyst, whose role is not too dissimilar to that of a psychoanalyst. Notice that, as the problem develops, it is necessary for the decision analyst to learn to understand the broker's attitude toward his problem as well as to understand the problem itself. It is frequently uncomfortable for a manager to consult a decision analyst because he must expose his attitudes and motivations toward the problem. Unless the analyst is able to understand the motivations of the manager as well as the objective characteristics of the problem, the full power of decision theory as a tool cannot be realized.

2.1 STRUCTURE OF THE PROBLEM

BROKER: Here's my problem as I see it. It is really quite simple, and we may be wasting each other's time by having you work on it, but a mistake would be costly. That's why I called you in. But before we discuss the problem, I must confess that I know nothing of decision analysis. Perhaps you should educate me a little bit first.

ANALYST: It will certainly be necessary for you to understand something about the principles of decision analysis if it is going to help you solve your problem. But that type of education can occur as the analysis develops. First, I want to make sure that I understand your problem as you described it in our telephone conversation. You have an opportunity to buy 100,000 tons of ore from a Far Eastern government for $5 per ton. If you are allowed to import it, you expect to be able to sell that ore for about $8 per ton, but if the government refuses to grant an import license, you will be forced to pay a penalty of $1 per ton. Is that right?

BROKER: That's about it. As I said, the facts are rather simple. I either make $300,000 profit or suffer a $100,000 loss.

ANALYST: We can start the analysis by drawing a simple decision tree. A decision tree is rather like a road map. It is a map of your decision problem and it includes only the events and your actions that are relevant to the problem. We will start the tree with an *act fork* that we represent by a small *box* with several branches emanating from it. Each branch represents one of the possible courses of action available to you now. In this case it appears that you only have two acts available—to buy the ore or not to buy the ore. Let the upper branch represent the decision Buy the Ore and the lower branch, the decision Don't Buy. I will use capital letters to label the act branches [see Figure 2–1].

Now start moving along the branch that indicates that you buy the ore. We will use an *event fork*, which has a *dot* rather than a box at the node, to represent the relevant consequences of that act. One possibility is that your application for an import license will be approved; you will then be $300,000 better off than you presently are. The upper branch of the event fork represents that potentiality. I will label it with lowercase letters. The other possibility, represented by the lower branch, is that your application for an import license will be rejected and you will lose $100,000. This too will be labeled with lowercase letters.

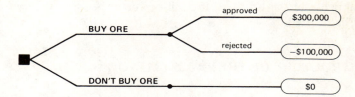

Figure 2–1   Broker's decision tree.

Finally, consider the other act branch—the one that corresponds to a decision not to buy the ore. Then there is only one event, and it represents neither a profit nor a loss. Thus its consequence is zero. Notice that I am using your present position as a base of zero from which to measure these consequences on each of the end branches of the tree.

2.2 PROBABILITIES

ANALYST: Your initial decision tree is now structured. The next step is to estimate a few probabilities. Do you think it is more likely that your application for a license will be approved or rejected?

BROKER: That's a tough question. I've had considerable experience in these matters, but it seems to me that such requests are rejected just about as often as they are approved.

ANALYST: Does that mean that you don't favor either outcome, not even by a little bit?

BROKER: I know which one I want to happen, but I can't decide which one is really more likely to happen. It's not that I don't know anything about it, but I honestly think that the government rejects about as many of these applications as it approves.

ANALYST: Fine. All I need is your carefully considered opinion. We will now assume, at least for a start, that the probability is .5 that your application will be approved and .5 that it will be rejected.

BROKER: Is that the same as the probability that I will get heads when I toss a coin?

ANALYST: Yes. You have said that if you apply for the license, you would be no more surprised if the government approved it than if it rejected it. Also, of course, if I were to toss a coin, you would be no more surprised if it came up heads than if it came up tails. We are going to use this .5 in analyzing the decision tree in the same way that we would use the same figure of .5 if a coin toss were really part of the problem we were analyzing. Let's look at that use now.

2.3   EXPECTED VALUE AND FOLDING BACK THE DECISION TREE

ANALYST: Now that the decision tree is structured in terms of act and event forks and evaluated in terms of both dollars and probabilities, we need to figure out the implication of these evaluations for the two initial courses of action. We call this process of evaluation *folding back.* We have labeled each of the end positions with what it is worth to you, with the net profit or loss that it represents. The goal of folding the tree back is to calculate what each of the initial acts is worth. It is rather easy in the case of the lower branch where you don't buy the ore. Not buying is followed only by a single event branch, and so the consequence of $0 can be folded back and labeled on the branch of not buying the ore. On the upper branch, where you do buy the ore, things are not quite so simple. The *value distribution* in Figure 2–2 displays your estimated probability distribution over the possible values that can result from buying the ore. Obviously, buying the ore must be worth some value that is between the two equally likely values, a $300,000 profit for the "approved" branch and a $100,000 loss for the "rejected" branch. The question is, What is that value?

We will use the concept of an *expected value (EV)* as a first approximation of what it is worth to buy the ore, that is, to represent with a single value what the entire value distribution in Figure 2–2 is worth. An expected value is a probability-weighted average. First, each possible value of the value distribution is weighted or multiplied by its associated probability and then these weighted values are summed. Thus .50 × −$100,000 = −$50,000; .50 × $300,000 = $150,000; and the sum = $100,000—the expected value of the distribution [Figure 2–3]. Of course, if someone else made different probability judgments from yours, his expected value would differ from yours. For example, if he estimated that the profit were more likely than the loss, his expected value would be greater than $100,000.

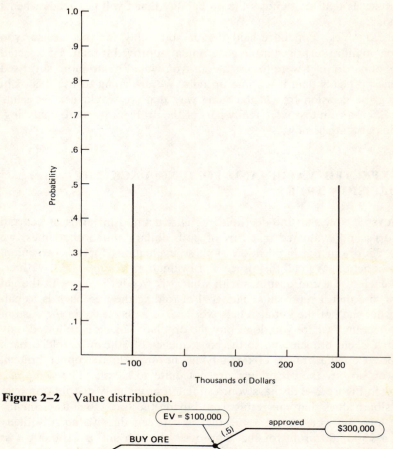

Figure 2–2   Value distribution.

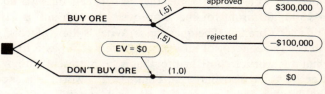

EV = expected value

Figure 2–3   Broker's decision tree.

BROKER: But what does it mean to calculate an expected value of $100,000?

ANALYST: We are after a single number that will represent the attractiveness of two numbers. Here we are interested in a single measure of profit or loss that will represent both the $300,000 profit and the $100,000 loss. I mentioned that the expected value is a special kind of mean; it is a probability-weighted average in that each of the profits or losses is weighted precisely by its probability of occurrence. Thus, like an ordinary mean, an expected value is a single measure intended to represent a set of scores. It is a number somewhere between the possible outcome of $300,000 profit and $100,000 loss. The reason that the expected value of $100,000 is exactly midway between the profit and loss is that your probability estimates in Figure 2–3 indicate that it is just as likely that the license will be approved as rejected.

Look at this scale in Figure 2–4 while I try to explain just how the probabilities influence an expected value. The scale extends from −$100,000 to $300,000, the two possible consequences if you decide to buy the ore. The expected value that we calculate on scale *A* is $100,000: .5 × $300,000 + .5 × −$100,000. Suppose that the probability you had estimated was different. Note what that does to the expected value. Suppose, for example, that you had estimated a probability of .75 for approval of the license and a probability of .25 for rejection. Now we are on the value distribution of scale *B*. The expected value is .75 × $300,000 + .25 × −$100,000, for a net of $200,000. This expected value is 75 percent of the distance away from the loss toward the profit because the profit is being weighted by a probability of .75. On scale *C* we will assume that you were much more pessimistic and had estimated only a 10 percent chance of a profit. Then the expected value would be .1 × $300,000 + .9 × −$100,000, for a net of −$60,000. The $60,000 expected loss is exactly 10 percent of the distance away from the $100,000 loss in the direction of the $300,000 profit.

This is what is meant by a probability-weighted average. Remember—*each of the dollar amounts entering into the expected value is weighted precisely by its probability of occurrence.* At this point, I would like you to figure out the expected value associated with your other course of action, where you do not buy the ore.

BROKER: But there are no profits or losses if I don't buy the ore. And there are no probabilities except . . . wait a minute. There is a probability of 1 that I will make $0 profit. If I multiply 1 by $0, my answer is $0. Is that the expected value?

ANALYST: Correct. The expected value of not buying the ore must be $0 because you are sure to make no profit.

Try a hypothetical example for practice in order to make sure that you understand what this expected value is. Imagine that you have the same 50 percent chance that you'll get the license and earn a $300,000 profit, but if the government rejects your license application, there is a chance that another brokerage firm would find the option attractive enough to be

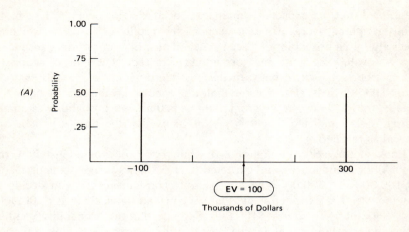

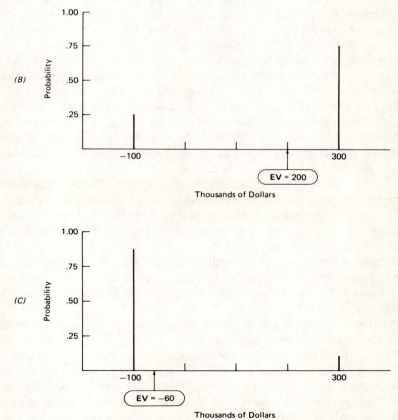

Figure 2–4   The influence of probability upon expected value.

willing to take the deal off your hands, in which case you would not be penalized the $100,000. Just imagine that there is a 30 percent chance of ending up with $0 profit (in the event that the other firm will assume your option) and a 20 percent chance of facing the $100,000 loss, and we still have the 50 percent chance of the $300,000 profit. Can you calculate the expected value of this more complex set of profit possibilities? The decision tree is sketched in Figure 2.5.

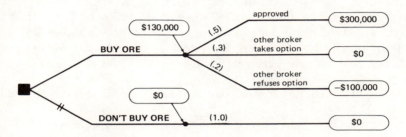

Figure 2–5   Expected value—three hypothetical events.

BROKER: We now have three different things that might happen. I guess that I just multiply each possible consequence by its probability and add up the products. That gives me $150,000 + $0 − $20,000; the expected value should be $130,000. [See Figure 2–5.]

ANALYST: Fine. This is probably a good time to stop doing arithmetic. Do you think the actual expected value figure of $100,000 that we calculated for your problem can help determine your decision?

BROKER: The $100,000 is a number that seems to be the right distance in between my profit or loss, assuming I buy the ore, but it is certainly not an amount of money that I will actually make. The expected value is a probability-weighted profit, but it isn't a number that is like an actual net profit, is it?

ANALYST: Your question shows a lot of insight. But I want to delay answering it. I would like you to assume, uncritically for now, that an expected value is a good measure of the attractiveness of an act and that it is a good policy to select whichever act has the highest expected value. Technically, you are following the policy of *maximizing expected value*. Thus you would buy the ore rather than not buy it because the expected value of $100,000 is more than the expected value of $0.

BROKER: I guess that makes sense.

ANALYST: Since you agree, I will use two short vertical lines to indicate that we will tentatively cross out the Don't Buy Ore act in the hypothetical case illustrated in Figure 2.5 as well as in your real problem shown in Figure 2.3.

2.4   SUBSEQUENT ACTS

ANALYST: It may be possible to find an act with a higher expected value. As I understand it, the reason you are in a hurry to buy, before applying for clearance, is that other brokers have the same option on the ore as you have.

BROKER: That is correct.

ANALYST: Are you sure that they would exercise their options? Maybe they find themselves in the same dilemma as you. How likely is it that the option would still be open if you waited for your approval to come through?

BROKER: Well, it's not very likely that it will still be open. I'm pretty sure that some other broker will buy the ore if I don't make a decision at once.

ANALYST: Well, just how sure are you? Do you think that it is impossible that it will be open?

BROKER: Oh no, but I would be quite surprised if it were open. I'm sure that the odds are better than 2 to 1 that someone else will buy the ore.

ANALYST: Are the odds as extreme as 3 to 1?

BROKER: Well, maybe not quite. That's pretty extreme.

ANALYST: Odds of 2 to 1 can be interpreted as implying two ways that the deal can be closed for every one way that it can be open. In other words, two out of three ways are closed. The probability is $2/(2 + 1)$ or .67. For odds of 3 to 1, there is a $3/(3 + 1)$ or .75 probability that someone else will buy the ore and close the deal.

BROKER: Then 70 percent sounds about right to me.

ANALYST: Okay, we will use 70 percent. Now we can evaluate the strategy of waiting. This strategy is represented by the Wait for Government Decision branch in Figure 2–6, the branch that indicates that you apply for clearance and do not exercise your option until after you find out whether or not your application is approved. Given approval of the application, there is from that point on the tree a 30 percent chance that you will successfully buy the ore and make $300,000 and a 70 percent chance that you will not. The subsequent acts of Buy Ore and Don't Buy are obvious choices at this point. Thus, conditional upon the license approval, the expected value is $90,000. It follows that the expected value of waiting for clearance is $45,000, considering that there is only a 50 percent chance that your application will be approved. Notice that I just took an expected value of an expected value when I used a .5 probability to weight the $90,000.

Here is the way that works. There are really three paths through the tree after waiting for a government decision. One is the sequence "approved, option open, Buy Ore." This entire path has a probability of, .15, which is the product of the component branch probabilities of .50 and .30. Thus, a probability of .15 is associated with a value of $300,000 in Figure 2–7.

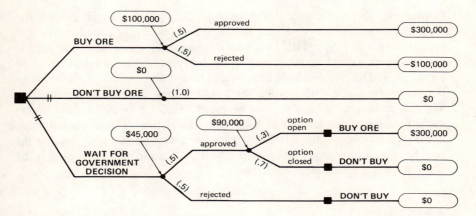

Figure 2–6   Wait for government decision.

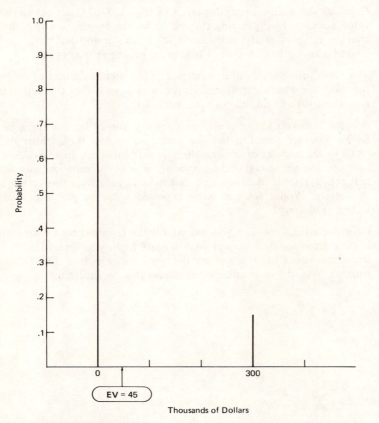

Figure 2–7   Expected value.

Continuing, there is a probability of .35 (.5 × .70) associated with the "approved, option closed, Don't Buy" path. This .35 is added to the .50 probability of the "rejected, Don't Buy" branch. Because both paths have end positions valued at $0, a total probability of .85 is attached to $0 in Figure 2–7. This yields an expected value of $45,000, which is the same as the value associated with waiting for a government decision in Figure 2–6. We will undoubtedly have further occasion to take expected values of expected values, which is kind of a shortcut calculation. This expected value is substantially below the $100,000 associated with immediately buying the ore. So we cannot improve upon the $100,000 expected value simply by waiting for the government decision.

ASSIGNMENTS

1. Consider the decision tree displayed in Figure 2–5. Calculate the expected value associated with buying the ore under the assumption that the broker changes his probability assessments to .2 for "approved," to .3 for "other broker takes option," and to .5 for "other broker refuses option."

2. The three probabilities must sum to 1. Find a combination of probabilities for the three events mentioned in problem 1 such that the expected value associated with buying the ore is exactly $0.

3. Assume that you are offered the following lottery for an entrance fee of $4.00. You are to roll a fair die once and receive the number of dollars equal to the number of dots on the side that turns up. In addition, if 4 dots turn up, you get to roll the die once again with the same payoffs as for the first roll. Draw the decision tree that models your opportunity to purchase the lottery. Would you maximize expected value by purchasing or by rejecting the lottery?

4. Consider a bet for which you win $10 if the reported high temperature for a week from today is greater than today's high; you lose $2.00 if the two highs are equal (to the nearest degree), and you lose $7.00 if today is warmer. Would you maximize expected value by accepting the bet?

3

THE ORE CASE:
INFORMATION AND
PROBABILITY ASSESSMENT

ANALYST: Before taking a more critical look at the policy of maximizing expected values, I want to make sure that we really have considered the entire problem. For example, other than waiting for a government decision, is there any way that you could obtain some information that would make you more certain about whether or not a request for an import license would be approved? However, before considering the information that you actually could obtain, I want to make some calculations that will give us an understanding of the potential value of any such information.

3.1 THE VALUE OF PERFECT INFORMATION

ANALYST: First, assume that you could act in a way to obtain *perfect information.* Suppose that you could get an accurate forecast, right now, about whether or not a license request would be approved. We will plug this hypothetical *information-seeking* action into your decision tree [see Figure 3–1]. We then have three initial acts on the tree—two branches for buying the ore and not buying the ore, which are the same as before, and a third act branch for getting free perfect information, in which case you will either "learn of approval" or "learn of rejection." These probabilities should each be .5 since you set the probability of approval at .5 and we have assumed that the information will be "learn of approval" if, and only if, the license would really be approved.

Following the "learning of approval" branch, you will decide either to buy or not to buy. If you buy, there is a probability of 1, since the information was perfect, that your application will be approved and a probability of

0 that it will be rejected. Therefore, the expected value associated with buying is 1 × $300,000, or $300,000. The expected value associated with not buying is still $0. Next, we will evaluate the "learn of rejection" branch. It is followed by an act fork with Buy and Don't Buy branches. If you buy, the probability is now 0 that your application will be approved and 1 that it will be rejected; therefore, the expected value associated with buying is a $100,000 loss, whereas the expected value associated with not buying is still $0.

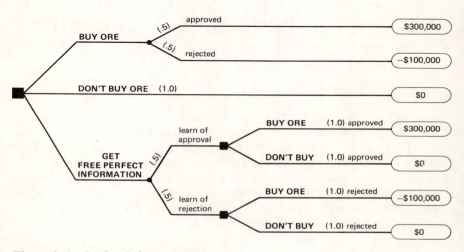

Figure 3–1   Perfect information.

Our tree is becoming complicated. After we structured the tree with a sequence of act forks and event forks, we evaluated it with respect to the value of getting to each of the end branches, which are technically called *end positions* since they represent the limit of this analysis. We then determined the probability to be attached to each event branch. Our next step is to calculate the implications of these probabilities and end point values for the initial act choices. Do they imply that you should buy the ore, not buy it, or get the perfect information? We are now folding back a rather complex tree and will make considerable use of the concept of expected value. But if we can assume, as we have just agreed, that you will always choose the course of maximizing expected value, at each act fork, then the process of folding back the tree is straightforward. We begin at the end points and then work our way back to the initial act branches by a series of expected value calculations.

The results of this process are displayed in Figure 3–2. We have already calculated the expected value of $100,000 and $0 for the first two courses of action. Next we will do it for the act of getting free perfect information. We begin by folding back the fourth from the bottom branch that is valued at $300,000. The probability of a license approval is 1, so we may simply use the $300,000 as an expected value, indicating the worth of traveling along the act branch of buying the ore. This expected value is indicated on the tree. Similarly an expected value of $0 is associated with not buying the ore after the "learn of approval" event. Let us continue back. The node following "learn of approval" has an expected value of $300,000, simply because we cut off and thereby delete the lower expected value associated with Don't Buy. If this node is worth an expected value of $300,000, then that is also the expected value associated with the branch "learn of approval." It is now necessary to calculate the expected value for the branch "learn of rejection." To make this calculation, it is necessary to return to the end position and again work backward.

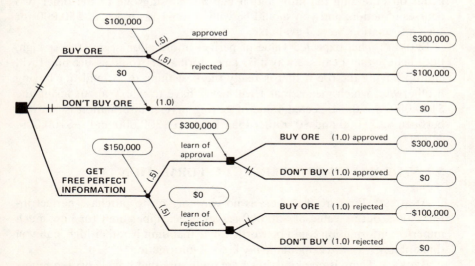

Figure 3–2 Perfect information—folding back.

The loss of $100,000 associated with the next to the bottom end position has a probability of 1. Thus the −$100,000 is carried directly back to its antecedent act of Buy Ore. Similarly, the profit of $0 associated with the bottom end position is carried directly back to the act branch Don't Buy. If we assume the policy of maximizing expected value, the node of the bottom act fork has an expected value of $0, which is higher than the $100,000 loss.

We are now in a position to calculate the expected value of the preceding branch, the position at which you are about to receive perfect information as to forthcoming approval or rejection. The expected value of this point is just the sum of the probability of .5 times the expected value of $300,000 associated with learning of approval, and the probability of .5 times the expected value of $0 associated with learning of rejection. This calculation yields an expected value of $150,000, which is midway between $0 and $300,000.

Earlier we noted that the expected value associated with the upper act of buying ore is $100,000 and the expected value associated with not buying the ore is $0. We have just calculated that the expected value associated with getting free perfect information is $150,000. Accordingly, if it were possible to get free perfect information, you would certainly do so. It has an expected value of $50,000 higher than the next best act. And that difference in expected value of $50,000 is what we define as the *value of obtaining perfect information*. From an expected value point of view, you are $50,000 better off obtaining the information before choosing one of the other two courses of action, and you should be willing to pay as much as $50,000 for such information, were it available.

BROKER: That expected value of perfect information seems rather high, but I believe that I can see why it is. The information would assure that I will end up buying the ore if that is really the best thing to do and not buying it otherwise, which means that I will never have to worry about losing the $100,000. So, the expected value of getting perfect information is halfway between $300,000 and $0, rather than between $300,000 and −$100,000.

3.2   THE VALUE OF IMPERFECT INFORMATION

ANALYST: I'm sure that there is no way for you to purchase perfect information, but its value of $50,000 serves as an upper limit for how much imperfect information could be worth. Since that limit is rather high, can you think of any way you can obtain any kind of information?

BROKER: There is one kind, but I am quite sure that it will cost too much. I know a Washington business consultant who would be willing to sound out the government position on importing ore from this Far Eastern country. The man is by no means infallible, but he has a pretty good record for this kind of thing. The problem is that he charges a fee of $1,000, and I expect that this is more than I should be willing to pay.

ANALYST: You are probably right, but it depends upon just how good you think this man is. I think that we should analyze the problem. Let me draw some more branches on the decision tree in Figure 3–3. If you use the expert, what will happen?

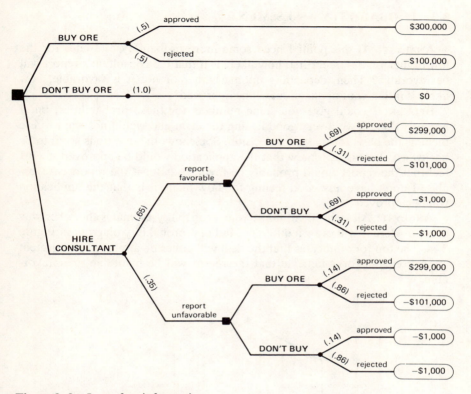

Figure 3-3 Imperfect information.

BROKER: He will either give me a favorable or an unfavorable report about what may happen to my application. He doesn't guarantee the accuracy of that report, but he is good.

ANALYST: All right, let's complete the tree then. We will start by adding one other initial act to the original acts of Buy versus Don't Buy. This act is to use the expert at a cost of $1,000. Your use of the expert will be followed by either a favorable or unfavorable report; in either case you will either buy or not buy the ore. Finally, the government will either approve or reject your application, and you will be faced with one of the consequences: $299,000 profit if you buy and the application is approved, $101,000 loss if you buy and the application is rejected, and $1,000 loss if you decide not to buy. Notice that each of these consequences is $1,000 less than in the case where you do not hire the consultant. Therefore, the only hope is that the increase in expected value due to the information purchased will more than offset the $1,000 cost of the information.

3.3 PROBABILITY ASSESSMENT

ANALYST: At this point I need some more probability estimates for the low branch on the tree. First, how likely is it that the consultant's report will be favorable? Then, depending upon whether or not it is favorable, how likely is it that your application will be approved?

BROKER: I could give you some numbers for those probabilities, but I honestly don't have a very good feeling for them and would not want to use them as the basis for making a decision. Somehow, the questions seem to be backward. That is, if I knew that the application would be approved, then I feel that the report would probably be favorable. But if the report is favorable, I don't have any good feeling for how likely it is that the application will be approved.

ANALYST: All right, then, make your probability estimates the other way around. Here, I will draw a different kind of a probability diagram in Figure 3–4. The top fork indicates that the deal will either be approved or rejected; the subsequent forks indicate that the report will be favorable or unfavorable.

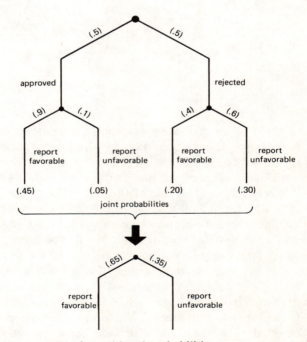

Figure 3–4   Assessment of conditional probabilities.

BROKER: I already said it is about equally likely that the application will be approved or rejected, so the first two probabilities are both .5.

In the case that the application will be approved, I feel quite certain that the consultant's report will be favorable. I will give an estimate of a 90 percent chance. That leaves a 10 percent chance that the report would be unfavorable. But I do not expect that the consultant will be able to gain as much information if it turns out that conditions are such that the application will be rejected. Therefore, I would estimate a 60 percent chance that his report will be unfavorable and a 40 percent chance that it will be favorable in that case.

ANALYST: I will take your probability assessments and do a little arithmetic on them. What you have estimated are called *unconditional probabilities* with respect to the approval of your request and *conditional probabilities* with respect to the favorability of each report. There is a theorem in probability theory that tells me that I can find the probability of any string of branches through the tree simply by multiplying all of the component probabilities together. Therefore, the probability that your application will be approved *and* that the report will be favorable is equal to .5 × .9, which is .45. Proceeding in a similar manner I find the probabilities of the other three paths are .05, .20, and .30. Note also that when I sum these *joint probabilities* for all end positions, the total is 1.

Now we have all of the ingredients necessary to calculate the probabilities needed for the first branch after Hire Consultant in Figure 3–3. First, the probability that the report will be favorable in case we use an expert, according to our calculations in Figure 3–4, is .45 + .20 = .65. That leaves a 35 percent chance of an unfavorable report.

Next, continue along the branch in Figure 3–3 in which the report is favorable. Regardless of whether or not you buy the ore, how likely is it that the application will be approved? As it turns out, you have already estimated the numbers that will permit us to calculate that probability. According to Figure 3–4, there is a .45 + .20 = .65 chance that the report will be favorable and a .45 chance that there will be both approval and a favorable report. According to the definition of a conditional probability, there is a .45/.65 = .69 chance of approval given a favorable report. It is as if 45 of the 65 ways (that is, 69 percent) in which the report can be favorable also include approval.

The same principle can be used to calculate the remaining probabilities in Figure 3–3. There is a .31 chance of rejection following a favorable report. If the report turns out to be unfavorable, there is a .05/(.05 + .30) = .14 chance of approval and a .30/(.05 + .30) = .86 chance of rejection.

BROKER: Let me look at those probabilities for a while. I want to be sure that I agree with them before we go further.

ANALYST: A good idea. You will observe that the probabilities that I have just written on the tree in Figure 3–3 are those that you felt uncomfortable about estimating. Instead, you estimated some other probabilities, and I derived the ones written down from those others that you estimated. Would you like to argue with any of these numbers?

BROKER: I am confused. These numbers might be okay and they might not. I am probably having difficulty challenging your calculated numbers for the same reason that I found it difficult to estimate them myself in the first place. Can we continue with the analysis, with some reservations about how "good" these numbers are?

ANALYST: That seems like a good idea. We will continue with these numbers and see whether you should hire the consultant or just go ahead and buy the ore without hiring him. Figure 3–5 indicates an expected value of $113,400 associated with hiring the consultant before deciding about buying the ore and an expected value of $100,000 if you buy the ore immediately.

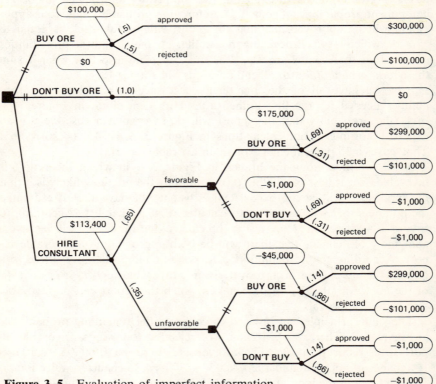

Figure 3–5 Evaluation of imperfect information.

Thus we can say tentatively that you're better off by $13,400 if you hire him.

3.4   SENSITIVITY ANALYSIS

BROKER: This result is starting to run counter to my intuition. Since I am still trying to understand how decision analysis works, I think that I would like to challenge your conclusions. I felt that $1,000 was too much to pay for the consultant; yet, this analysis suggests that I am $13,400 better off if I hire him than if I don't.

ANALYST: I agree with your point about challenging everything you don't understand; unless you accept almost everything that goes on in the analysis, you probably won't allow the results to affect your final decision very much. Now, about the consultant. Why did the alternative of using him increase our expected value so much? Let's consider the decision tree in Figure 3–5. It seems that while $1,000 may be a lot of money, it is a rather small amount in relation to the difference between the $300,000 profit and the $100,000 loss. The information that you get from the consultant helps you make a better decision about buying the ore and thus changes the probabilities that weight these large consequences. To put it another way, the additional information enables you to make a better decision under uncertainty, increasing the expected payoff associated with that decision.

BROKER: But the probabilities on that part of the tree are those with which I was quite uncomfortable. I am still hesitant about paying that $1,000, primarily because I felt so uneasy about the probabilities that imply that I should hire the consultant.

ANALYST: Then we should find out just how important those probabilities are to this conclusion. We can run what is called a *sensitivity analysis* on them. Thus far we have made a kind of miniature model of your problem, and you don't feel very comfortable with some of the probabilities in that model. So, let's change the model in order to find out what happens in the conclusion; that is, we will modify the probabilities that you estimated in Figure 3–4 and calculate the resulting impact on the expected value associated with hiring a consultant.

Consider once again the probabilities that you estimated in Figure 3–4. Which ones are you least sure of?

BROKER: Well, I'm certainly prepared to live with the .5-.5 probabilities for approval versus rejection, so I guess it has to be some of the other probabilities.

ANALYST: Then about the only thing you could be wrong on is your estimate of the information value in the consultant's report. What happens to the expected value if we vary the information content of his report and you know how it varies?

First, let's "improve" the consultant. What if you knew that his information were perfect? In that case you would correctly purchase the ore if your application were to be approved and correctly not buy it if your application were to be rejected. There is a 50 percent chance of approval, in which case you would make a net profit of $299,000, and a 50 percent chance of rejection, which would lead to the $1,000 loss representing the amount you paid the consultant. The expected value, therefore, is $149,000. This is entirely consistent with our earlier calculation that the expected value associated with free perfect information was $150,000. Consequently, if you actually knew that the consultant was perfect, it would be worth a lot more than $1,000 to hire him. In fact, this analysis implies that it should be worth up to $50,000. If your probability estimates in Figure 3–4 err on the conservative side, there is no problem. If the consultant turns out to be better than you think he is, then you still want to hire him.

But what if you knew he was not quite as good as is implied by the probabilities in Figure 3–4? To reflect this, we would have to make the conditional probabilities less extreme. Let us follow the "approved" branch. What is the least extreme probability of a favorable report that is reasonable?

BROKER: Well, that is where I think that he is good at correctly finding out that the license would be approved. But we could push that probability from 90 percent down to 80 percent just to see what happens.

ANALYST: Fine. I will make that change in Figure 3–6. Next, assume that we are on the "rejected" branch. Can we make the 60 percent probability associated with an unfavorable report less extreme?

BROKER: If I were to move the probability of a favorable report back to 50 percent, then the consultant would be just as likely to give a favorable as an unfavorable report in the event that my application were to be rejected.

ANALYST: That's right.

BROKER: No, that doesn't make sense. In fact, I was probably hedging a little bit when I made the 60–40 estimate.

ANALYST: Then 60–40 will remain in Figure 3–6. I will apply those probabilities to your decision tree, which is now in Figure 3–7, and then calculate the resulting expected values. Your new probability estimate implies an expected value of only $99,000 if you hire the consultant. That is $1,000 less than the expected value resulting from buying the ore immediately.

BROKER: Then I shouldn't hire him?

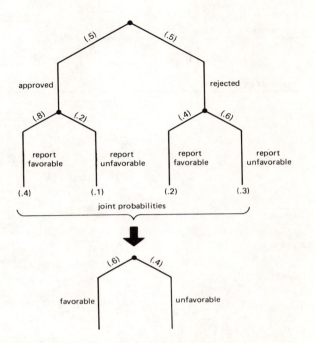

Figure 3–6   Reassessment of conditional probabilities.

ANALYST: We need to examine the probabilities a little more before coming to a firm conclusion. First, I think I see why the expected value dropped to $99,000. Ignore the $1,000 fee for a moment. If the report is unfavorable, these probabilities indicate that it is exactly three times as likely that your application will be rejected as approved. On the other hand, the $300,000 profit is exactly three times as great as the $100,000 loss. These reversed ratios of probabilities and profits offset each other exactly, and so, after an unfavorable report, Buy and Don't Buy have the same expected value. This means that the evidence just misses being strong enough to force you not to buy after an unfavorable report, and, of course, you buy after a favorable report. If you end up buying the ore regardless of the outcome of the report, then hiring the consultant is essentially the same as wasting his fee of $1,000.

To continue the sensitivity analysis, we will calculate the manner in which the expected value changes as I push the probability of a favorable report given approval from .8 back to .9. It increases along the straight line drawn in Figure 3–8 as the probability increases.

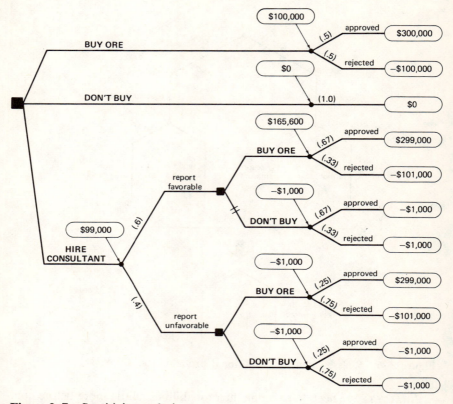

Figure 3–7   Sensitivity analysis.

BROKER: That expected value certainly does move up a lot as the probability moves toward .9. And the more we discuss that probability, the more convinced I become that 90 percent is a good estimate. It just has to be very likely that the consultant would write a favorable report if it were the case that the application would be approved.

I am beginning to change my mind about the consultant. The $1,000 fee doesn't look so large anymore, particularly with the very large possible profits or losses. I am increasingly anxious to cut down the possibility of that $100,000 loss. Perhaps I should call the consultant this afternoon. I don't want to lose any time that would permit another broker to buy the ore.

ANALYST: Wait just a minute. Even if you are sure about that 90 percent probability, you'll want to buy the ore only if you agree with the policy of maximizing expected value. Before calling the consultant, we should spend more time in order to take a long, hard look at what these expected dollars really mean. And we should also ask whether there are any other parts of this analysis about which you may have critical uncertainty.

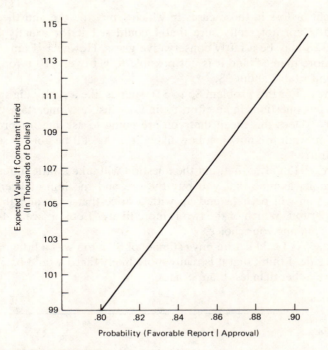

Figure 3–8   Sensitivity analysis.

3.5   UNCERTAIN QUANTITIES

ANALYST: Before asking whether you really want to maximize expected value, we need to examine the end positions of the tree in order to make sure that you really believe in the values we ascribed to them. In particular, which end branches describe amounts of dollars that you will receive for sure, and which ones describe amounts that you are uncertain about?

BROKER: Do you want me to look through the entire tree?

ANALYST: That's right. Check out Figure 3–5 again.

BROKER: Well, let's see. For the branch in which I don't buy and I haven't spent any money, I know for sure that the final outcome is $0. For the branches where I don't buy after having spent $1,000 on the consultant, I know for sure that the final loss is $1,000. I am also sure that the penalty associated with buying the ore and then having my application for a license turned down is $100,000—so that means that I am sure of a $100,000 loss if I don't use an expert, buy the ore, and my application is rejected. I am also sure of a $101,000 loss if my application is rejected after I have consulted an expert and purchased the ore. However, I am uncertain about the exact profit or loss in those cases in which I buy the ore and the license is approved. I am not really sure that I could sell it for exactly $8 a ton. Actually, $8 may be a fairly conservative guess. However, I am sure that I can get more than $5 and it is not possible to get over $10 a ton; so I feel rather comfortable about $8.

ANALYST: For this problem $5 to $10 sounds like a pretty big spread. Let me ask a few questions in an effort to find out just how uncertain you are.

BROKER: Does this mean that you are going to ask me for probabilities again? You want to know just how likely it is that I'll be able to sell the ore for $8 a ton?

ANALYST: I'm after that, but the question will take a little different form. For example, assume that you buy the ore and the import license comes through. You will perhaps end up with a price that is greater than or less than $8 per ton. Which of the two is more likely? Look at scale *A* in Figure 3–9 while making your choice.

BROKER: As I said before, my estimate of $8 a ton was a little on the conservative side. I think that it is really more likely that I would be able to sell it for more rather than less than $8 a ton.

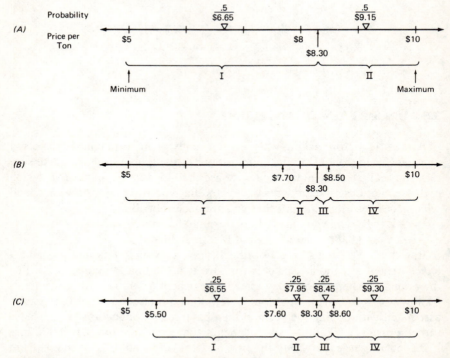

Figure 3–9 Assessment of uncertain quantities (probability assigned to interval midpoints).

ANALYST: Fine. Now I want to push your estimates around. Do you think that it is more likely that you would end up selling it for more or less than $8.20 a ton?

BROKER: That's getting pretty tough. But I think it is just a little more likely that I would sell it for more than $8.20.

ANALYST: How about $8.40?

BROKER: That figure is close too, but I expect that it is a little more likely that I would sell it for less than $8.40 than for more.

ANALYST: $8.30?

BROKER: I give up. I am too confused to make a choice in that region. More than $8.30 a ton is just as likely as less than $8.30 a ton. I guess that's the figure that I should have given you the first time?

ANALYST: No, not necessarily. In fact, it is beginning to look as though $8 was a pretty good approximation. But let me ask a few more questions to test how uncertain you are about that $8.30. What we have done so far is divide the entire continuum of price per ton into two intervals that are equally likely. You have said that it is just as likely that you will sell the ore for more than $8.30 a ton as for less. I want to take those two ranges and divide each of them into two intervals that are also equally likely. First, ignore the range above $8.30 a ton. Look at scale *B* in Figure 3–9 and decide whether you think that it is more likely that you will sell the ore for less than $7 or for between $7 and $8.30?

BROKER: It is much more likely that I will sell it for more than $7.

ANALYST: You think that it is more likely that you will sell it for between $7 and $8.30 than for less than $7?

BROKER: Sure.

ANALYST: Okay. Now increase the amount. Do you think that it is more likely that you will sell it for less than $7.50 or for between $7.50 and $8.30?

BROKER: That's a tough choice, but I would still bet on the interval between $7.50 and $8.30.

ANALYST: How about $7.70?

BROKER: I am just about indifferent there. Any finer movements would be merely guesswork.

ANALYST: Let us consider the high range. This time ignore the range below $8.30 per ton. Do you think that it is more likely that the price will fall between $8.30 and $9 or above $9 a ton?

BROKER: Between $8.30 and $9.

ANALYST: Between $8.30 and $8.50 or above $8.50?

BROKER: Leave the marker at $8.50. I am just about indifferent there.

ANALYST: Fine. We have made a first pass at dividing the price continuum into four equally likely intervals, but we are probably not home yet. Consider the four intervals in scale *B* of Figure 3–9: below $7.70, between

$7.70 and $8.30, between $8.30 and $8.50, and above $8.50. I would like you to choose the interval that you think is most likely to contain the actual selling price for ore.

BROKER: I probably shouldn't be able to choose between them if they are all equally likely.

ANALYST: Theoretically, that is right. But we are trying to get a closer and closer approximation to your carefully considered judgment about these uncertainties. Which of the intervals looks best?

BROKER: I know that this is being inconsistent with my previous choices, but, for some reason or other, both middle intervals look a little less likely than the extremes. I wouldn't choose either of those.

ANALYST: That's what I expected. When people make judgments like the ones that you have been making, there is frequently a tendency for them to feel a little too committed to the middle number, and, consequently, I am not surprised that you felt a bit of a tendency to squeeze in a little too close to the $8.30.

BROKER: That must have been it. Try pushing those outer markers in scale *C* of Figure 3–9 out to $7.60 and $8.60. There, that's better. Now I can't make a choice.

ANALYST: Then let's try this test. Suppose I select any two intervals that I want, and leave you with the other two. If the price of ore falls in the intervals I've chosen, you pay me $100; if not, I'll pay you $100. Does this seem like a fair deal to you?

BROKER: I guess so because if I were to have the first choice, I really don't know which intervals I would pick.

ANALYST: Good. Let me ask some other questions. A few moments ago you said you were sure that the price per ton would not be less than $5 nor more than $10. Can you give me a better estimate? I would like to pick the narrowest extremes possible, such that you are sure that the price would not fall outside these limits.

BROKER: Well, the $10 figure looks good, but the $5 estimate is perhaps a little conservative. I am absolutely sure that the price of ore will not fall below $5.50.

ANALYST: Good. That gives me all the information I need. Now I will sketch out, in Figures 3–10 and 3–11 two different kinds of probability distributions that will serve as alternative displays of your assessments. The distribution in Figure 3–10 is called a cumulative probability distribution. The vertical coordinate refers to the probability that the price per ton will be equal to or less than the amount indicated on the horizontal coordinate. Notice the small dots on the graph. Your assessments in scale *C* of Figure 3–9 indicate that there is a zero probability that the price will be less than $5.50, a .25 chance that the price will be less than $7.60, a .50 chance that it will be less than $8.30, a .75 chance that it will be less than $8.60, and a probability of one that it will be less than $10. I simply connected those dots by the smooth curve in the graph.

BROKER: I understand where you got the dots and curve, but the cumulative probability doesn't communicate much to me. The original intervals in scale *C* of Figure 3–9 are more meaningful.

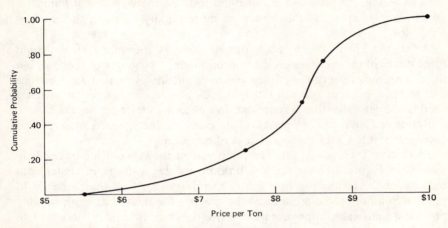

Figure 3–10   Cumulative probability function.

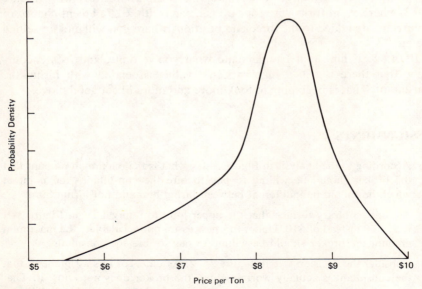

Figure 3–11   Probability density function.

ANALYST: That's what I was afraid of, so I transformed Figure 3–10 to what is technically called a probability density function in Figure 3–11. The *height* of the density function is simply equal to the *change* in the cumulative probability. Notice how the density function is quite high in the region of $8.50 per ton where the cumulative probability increases most sharply.

BROKER: The density curve resembles the bell-shaped curves that I am used to seeing. And it looks about right, too . . . the way that it humps in about the right spot and then drops off more rapidly on the high side than on the low.

ANALYST: Then let's stay with your assessments in Figure 3–9. We could place either of these curves on the appropriate end positions of the tree, but there is a simpler procedure. Since you have already estimated a .25 chance that the true price of ore will fall into each of those four intervals, what I need is a single value that is representative of each of the four intervals.

BROKER: Can't you simply take the center value of each interval and assume that it has a 25 percent chance of happening?

ANALYST: Technically, no. The midpoints of the two outside intervals in scale *C* of Figure 3–9 are really a little bit too far away from center. But because of the estimation bias that I mentioned earlier—the tendency to squeeze in a little too close around the center—the midpoints will probably provide a reasonable approximation. Since the error isn't large, and the two kinds of biases should tend to offset each other, I will go ahead and use the midpoints as representative of each interval. This permits me to draw Figure 3–12, where event forks with four events, each with a 25 percent chance of occurring, are added to the three end positions where you will end up selling the ore.

BROKER: I think that I understand what you've done, and it is encouraging that there is still a high expected value associated with hiring the consultant. That is beginning to look more and more like a good move.

ASSIGNMENTS

1.   According to the analysis in Figure 3–12, what is the maximum amount that the broker should be willing to pay to hire the consultant—the point at which he should be indifferent between hiring him and not hiring him?

2.   Assume, contrary to fact, that the upper limit to interval IV in Figure 3–9 is $12.60 instead of $10. Under this new assumption, calculate the maximum amount the broker should be willing to pay to hire the consultant.

3.   Consider the decision tree in Figure 3–12. Assume, for this assignment, that the consultant is actually worthless, but the broker does not know it. That is, assume that the consultant is really just as likely as not (probability = .5) to make a favorable report, regardless of whether the application will

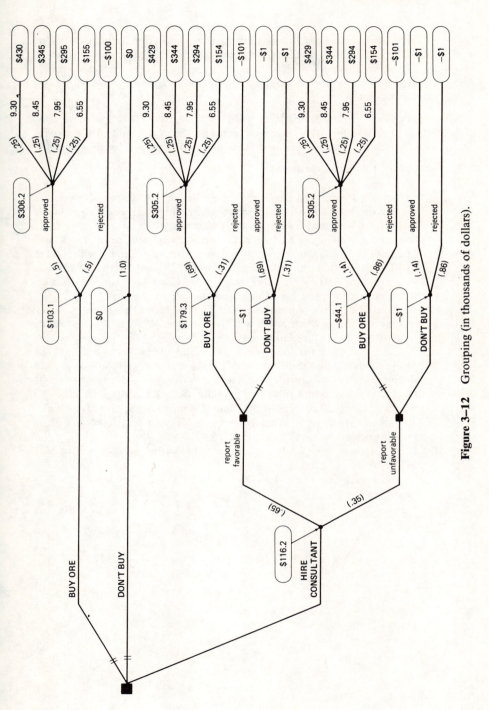

Figure 3–12 Grouping (in thousands of dollars).

be approved or rejected. But assume that the broker makes his decisions under the assumption of his current probability estimates with respect to the consultant's report. Calculate what happens to the expected values associated with the three initial acts. Would the broker agree with your expected values? Explain.

4. Consider the probability diagram in Figure 3–4. If we assume those *conditional* probabilities of a favorable report, what probability of approval would yield a 50 percent *unconditional* probability of a favorable report?

5. Answer the following questions:

   a. Robert A. Landis has a chance to participate in a special game. A regular die is to be tossed. If one, two, or three turn up, a drawing is made from a bag with three black and seven white balls in it. If four, five, or six turn up, a ball is drawn from a bag with seven black and three white balls in it. If the ball drawn is black, Landis will receive $100. If it is white, he will have to pay $85. Landis is risk-neutral. It will cost him $10 to play this game if he elects to. Using a decision tree, demonstrate whether or not he should play the game.

   b. An infallible clairvoyant offers to tell Landis before he decides whether to play the game whether he will win or lose. What is the maximum Landis should pay the clairvoyant?

   c. Mr. Landis fails to do business with the clairvoyant, but his kid brother, who is not infallible, offers his services. For $10 he will predict the number that will turn up on the die. Looking into the brother's past record, you assess the following probabilities. If the die falls high, he forecasts "low" 20 percent of the time. If it falls low, he forecasts "high" 50 percent of the time. What is the probability he will forecast high if Landis engages his services?

   d. If he forecasts "low," what is the probability that the die will in fact fall high?

   e. Should Landis pay the clairvoyant's brother $10 for his services?

4

THE ORE CASE:
TIME, CRITERIA, AND UTILITY

ANALYST: We have been acting as if the dollar amount assigned to each of the end positions tells how pleased or displeased you would be to land on that point. But, this is seldom the situation. We must now take a close look at other differences between the outcomes. For example, the dollar amounts we have been using represent the net cash flow from now until you get to the end position. However, the timing of these cash flows may, in itself, be important. Also, there may be some consequences that are not practical to measure directly in money terms. Some firms, for instance, have been reluctant to undertake ventures with a substantial expected value because it is too costly in terms of public relations, employee morale, or aggravation. These adverse effects generally are thought of as impairing future cash flows and profits in ways that may be very hard to figure.

Finally, I would like you to look at your attitude toward risk. Decisions that are sound when accompanied by a large capital backing may be unwise for a smaller firm with less capital, mainly because of the degree of risk involved. In this vein, you will recall that the expected value associated with buying the ore is not an amount that can actually be realized. Instead, you will receive substantially more than the expected value if the license is approved but much less than the expected value if the application is rejected. There are tools for handling such issues, and we will now apply some of them to your problem to see whether our preliminary conclusion, that you should hire the consultant, should be altered in light of these additional factors.

4.1 ACCOUNTING FOR TIME

ANALYST: Our first step is to ensure that all the cash flows figured into our evaluation actually will occur at about the same point in time. *When* will the various amounts of money change hands?

BROKER: If I hire a consultant, $1,000 will be payable immediately. The actual transactions on the ore itself, however, will take place over a three-year period. If I buy the ore, I will contract right now to pay $5 a ton for it. Then, right after receiving my license, I will contract with a purchaser to sell him the ore at some fixed price, such as $8 a ton or whatever the market happens to be at that time. The entire deal will be made almost immediately, but the transactions will not occur until sometime in the future. It happens that the ore will be received in three separate shipments—one will be received now, one in six months, and the final one in one year. I will pay for each shipment at the same time as I receive payment, and so it is unnecessary to borrow any money.

ANALYST: You don't have to pay any interest, but do you mean that all of the cash transactions will not be complete until a year from now?

BROKER: Right. That's pretty typical of deals like this.

ANALYST: Then it will be necessary for us to calculate *present values* for the amounts at the end positions of the tree. For example, consider the top branch. What is the value today of a $430,000 profit that will be received in the three equal semiannual payments? What is today's cash equivalent to you of those three installments of profit? How much would you require today in exchange for giving up those future payments?

BROKER: Let's assume a 5 percent semiannual interest rate.

ANALYST: Fine, I have some tables that show, at that rate, that the present value of the $430,000 is only $409,900, so now we will replace all of the dollars at the end positions with their respective present values in Figure 4–1.

BROKER: Wow! That sure lowers the expected values.

ANALYST: And so it should. Our earlier analysis was based on my faulty assumption that you would receive the profit immediately.

4.2 NONMONETARY CRITERIA

ANALYST: Are there any factors, other than time and its effect on the value of money, that should cause adjustments to the values at the end positions?

BROKER: As far as I am concerned, money is almost everything in this business. Let's see, things that do not involve money—that's a tough question. Maybe this is important. Deals like this often open up opportunities for later business; actually, I was offered this particular option as a result of having recently purchased a different commodity from the same Far Eastern government. But this consideration seems a little vague to be incorporated into a quantitative decision tree. Still, I suppose we could add more branches, indicating whether or not such an opportunity would occur.

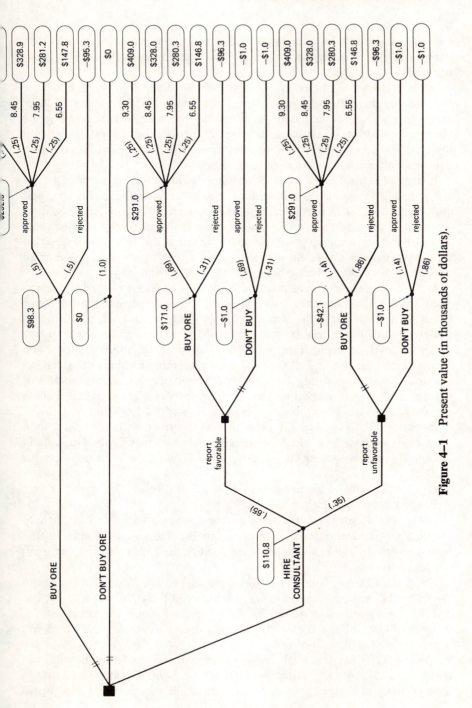

Figure 4–1 Present value (in thousands of dollars).

I don't really know how much such an opportunity would be worth. Perhaps there would be more than one. The situation can get awfully complicated.

ANALYST: Adding more branches certainly would be possible, but if we keep adding them, the tree might become more of a hindrance than a help. At some point in the analysis it is necessary to make side calculations or simply to make rough intuitive judgments and then incorporate them into the quantitative analysis, formally or informally. For now, I think it is best that we don't add too much more to the tree.

Instead, I want you to consider, intuitively, the value of possible future deals arising from this one. In order to make an intuitive evaluation, you must understand the concept of a *selling price*. A selling price is a way of estimating how much something is worth to you. Actually, the present value is something like a selling price. It can be viewed as the answer to a question such as "How much would someone have to pay you now in order to purchase your right to the $300,000 three months from now?"

Let's estimate the selling price of future deals. Try to imagine the expected value of these deals. Using your past experience, make a judgment about what such potential contacts are worth to your business. Suppose someone you'd never seen before and would never see again offered to buy all rights to these deals from you today. Suppose he offered to pay you $1,000, now, in cash in exchange for your presenting to him exclusively all opportunities that you might obtain as a result of your having made this current deal. I understand that this is a very hypothetical situation, but do you think you would be willing to sell these rights for $1,000?

BROKER: That's hard to say. The $1,000 is attractive, but I would soon go out of business if I couldn't continue to generate new deals. No, I don't believe I would be willing to sell the potential future business contacts for $1,000.

ANALYST: Well how much would it take, $2,000?

BROKER: I would sell for $3,000.

ANALYST: Remember, I am not asking you for a figure that you would consider a good deal or the best price obtainable. I am after the amount that would just make you *indifferent* between selling the rights and keeping them for your own use.

BROKER: Oh! Just like when you were asking questions that led up to that probability distribution. Well, I wouldn't sell the rights for $2,000, but I would gladly sell them for $3,000. So, I guess I would be just about indifferent about selling for $2,500 cash on the line. At that price I wouldn't care whether I sold them or not.

ANALYST: Then that is the number we will use, and this amount will make the deal look more attractive than before. I will simply add $2,500 to each of the end points that follow your purchase of the ore. To be worth the $2,500, does it make any difference whether or not your license is approved?

BROKER: Oh, that's right. I had been assuming that the entire transaction was successful. Actually, if I end up reneging on my purchase of the ore, my reputation will be damaged. We really should assess a penalty for the bad branches if we are giving a bonus of $2,500 to the end positions where I've had a successful deal.

ANALYST: The penalties are probably a little more difficult to assess. Is there any way you can put a dollar figure on the expected harm that would result from a rejected application? It is like estimating the most that you will be willing to pay for an insurance policy if someone else would agree to pick up the pieces in case something bad happens to you.

BROKER: That analogy doesn't quite fit because there is no way for someone else to repair this kind of damage, but I understand what you are after. The damage is probably less serious than the expected gain if all goes well. I guess that I will be just about indifferent about the prospect of paying a $500 insurance premium to guarantee against the damages to future business losses. But there is something else at stake. It is personally embarrassing to have to back down on a deal. This cost is kind of a "cocktail party discomfort." But it is about as important to me as the loss of future business. I guess that means a total of a $1,000 downward adjustment if I am forced to back down on the deal.

ANALYST: Fine. Therefore, in Figure 4–2 I will simply add $2,500 to the "good" branches and subtract $1,000 from each of the "bad" ones. Can you think of any other criteria that we should adjust for?

BROKER: I don't think so. It may be worth a little bit to have some experience with the consultant, but not much. It is probably too trivial to be included in this analysis, and I really can't think of anything else.

ANALYST: Then, let's consider the problem of risk.

4.3 ANALYSIS OF ATTITUDE TOWARD RISK

ANALYST: Figure 4–2 makes the decision to hire the consultant look rather obvious if you are neutral toward taking risks and adopt the policy of maximizing expected value. However, that may not be the best decision if you can't take the chance of losing money or if, perhaps, you really like to gamble.

BROKER: I most certainly do not want to gamble. In fact, that is primarily why I called you in the first place. I am generally more cautious than my competitors on all sorts of transactions. Even though I can borrow money when it is well secured, my business is not in very good shape in terms of working capital. Otherwise, I probably would have purchased the ore without ever having called you.

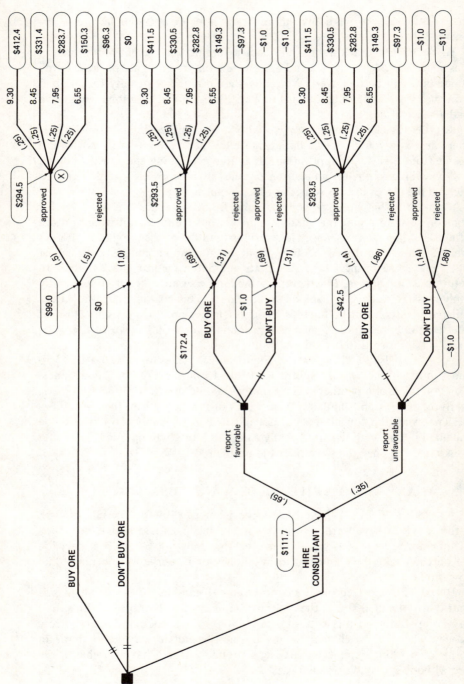

Figure 4–2 Nonmonetary criteria (in thousands of dollars).

ANALYST: Then it is appropriate, as our next and final step, to incorporate your attitude toward risk into the decision analysis. I will start by asking you for some more selling prices. Consider, first, the point labeled X in the tree in Figure 4–2, where you have a 25 percent chance of making profits that we have converted into each of four present values. According to the figure the expected value of those present values is $294,500. Perhaps the gamble facing you, if you were at point X, is not worth the expected value. It would be if your attitude toward risk were neutral, but you have just said that you want to avoid risk. Therefore, I expect that the gamble is worth something less than $294,500 to you.

BROKER: I don't really view it as a gamble. In fact, none of my business transactions are gambles. I always consider my alternatives carefully and use a lot of past experience in making my decisions.

ANALYST: Perhaps the word gamble is a poor choice of terms; I didn't mean it to have any negative connotations. The point is that you can end up with any one of those four present value profits and you don't know which one you will win. Just bear with me a while and assume that you have a gamble whenever you are not sure what the final outcome will be. What I need next from you is a selling price for that gamble with four outcomes; and, because of your cautious attitude toward risk, your selling price should be somewhat less than the expected value.

Imagine that an insurance company will be willing to take the risk off your hands. Assume, for example, that you were at this point, that is, that you had purchased the ore and your license had been approved. The only uncertainty remaining is the price at which you can sell the ore. Given that assumption, how much would an insurance company have to pay you, right now, in exchange for the privilege of receiving whichever one of the profits is actually realized?

BROKER: Oh, I see what you are after. This is another one of those selling prices where I am indifferent about whether or not I actually sell it. You say that my selling price should be somewhat less than the expected value? Just why is that?

ANALYST: Well, there is some risk involved whenever you don't know which of the profits or losses you would actually earn; and since you wish to avoid risk, you should be willing to pay a premium in order to induce someone else to take that risk off your hands and to give you a *certain* price for the ore.

BROKER: So, the amount by which my selling price is less than the expected value is a kind of risk premium?

ANALYST: Exactly.

BROKER: This is a difficult judgment to make. I would sell that gamble, as you call it, for something less than the highest profit and for more than the smallest profit. I guess it also makes sense that I should sell it for less than its expected value of $294,500, but not much less. For now, I guess I would sell it for about $275,000, but I don't want you to hold me to that; I may change my mind later on.

ANALYST: That's okay. We'll make a more careful assessment later. I can get by with a tentative number for the present. I need it only to illustrate what we will be doing. I want to use an amount like the $275,000 to replace the expected value at point X in Figure 4–2. We now want to replace all expected values with what the respective points on the tree are worth. Since you like to be cautious, the replacement amounts should generally be smaller than the expected values.

These replacement amounts are special kinds of selling prices that are sometimes called *certainty equivalents*. The first thing I want to do is replace those three end forks that have four branches with their certainty equivalents, with the single dollar amounts that are equivalent to each of the forks. Then we will continue to fold back the tree by replacing expected values with certainty equivalents all the way back to the beginning. This process will yield a measure of worth for each of the initial acts—a measure that is appropriately adjusted to account for your attitude toward risk.

BROKER: Does that mean that you want me to assess selling prices for every single chance fork on the decision tree?

ANALYST: I would have you do that if it were not such a difficult task.

BROKER: I agree. That would be a difficult task.

ANALYST: Relax. Instead, I am going to ask you for your selling price, or certainty equivalent, for a much simpler gamble; then use that to calculate all of the certainty equivalents throughout the decision tree.

BROKER: How can you do that?

ANALYST: I'll show you. What is the maximum profit you could make according to Figure 4–2?

BROKER: The highest present value is $412,400.

ANALYST: Fine. What is the maximum possible loss?

BROKER: $97,300.

ANALYST: Right. I am going to draw a graph that will have along the horizontal axis all amounts from −$97,300 to $412,400.

I will now take a quarter out of my pocket. On a fair toss it is just as likely to come up heads as it is tails. I think you will begin to understand why I have been calling these chance forks gambles. I want you to evaluate the certainty equivalent of a much simpler gamble than any of those involved in the decision tree. If I flip this coin and it comes up heads, you will win $412,400. But if it comes up tails, you will lose $97,300.

BROKER: This is a serious gamble.

ANALYST: What is your certainty equivalent?

BROKER: As I said earlier, I would love to win $412,400 but it would be rough on my business if I were to lose the $97,300.

ANALYST: As a guide, this 50-50 gamble has an expected value of $157,550.

BROKER: I suppose that means that my certainty equivalent should be somewhat less than $157,550. In fact, it is much less!

ANALYST: Can you give me a good firm estimate of how much less?

BROKER: [*After considerable hesitation*] I will settle on a firm selling price of $25,000. If you actually offered me that gamble at this moment, and I didn't have the ore deal pending, I would be willing to sell the gamble for $25,000.

ANALYST: Now I will show you the utility function that I am constructing in Figure 4–3. The horizontal axis represents dollars; the vertical axis, utility. *Utility* is kind of a personal value of dollars to you. At this point I can start to fill in Figure 4–3. I will let the utility scale extend from 0 to 1. The actual figures I use are arbitrary. Next, I will let 0 utiles be worth −$97,300 because that is the least attractive of all of the outcomes; 1 utile is worth $412,400, because that is the most attractive of all the outcomes; and, .5 utile is worth $25,000. Now I will draw the smoothest curve that I can through these three points.

BROKER: Go on.

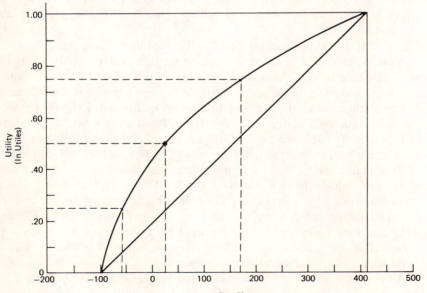

Figure 4–3   Utility.

ANALYST: You will recall that the gamble was that you would win $412,400 if heads turned up and −$97,300 if tails turned up. Now switch from the dollar scale; on the utility scale you would win 1 utile if heads turned up and 0 utiles if tails turned up. Furthermore, that gamble should be equal to its expected utility or .50 utile. The expected utility is calculated just as an expected value on the utility scale: $(.50 \times 1) + (.50 \times 0)$, which is equal to .50 utile.

BROKER: This is confusing.

ANALYST: I can appreciate that, but try to stay with me for a while longer. I next want to check out this utility function by asking you if you will agree to two other certainty equivalents. Suppose that you own a gamble where you win $25,000 if heads turn up and $97,300 if tails turn up. On your utility function this gamble has an expected utility of .25. The associated number of dollars is −$55,000. That means, if this is a good utility function, that you should be just willing to pay a $55,000 insurance premium to avoid a 50-50 chance of either losing $97,300, or winning $25,000.

BROKER: [*Again after some hesitation*] That price seems reasonable. I will not argue with it at all, again assuming I didn't have the ore deal in front of me.

ANALYST: Good. Then there is only one more check. This time, heads you win $412,400, and tails, you win $25,000. That gamble has an expected utility of .75, and the associated selling price is $170,000. Is that also reasonable?

BROKER: [*More hesitation*] Yes, I will accept that selling price.

ANALYST: Next I want to do something that will probably seem like number magic to you. According to utility theory, since you have claimed by several estimates to be conservative, it is inappropriate to do arithmetic by calculating expected values on a dollar scale. Instead, I should be doing that arithmetic on a utility scale. Therefore, I will draw a new decision tree in Figure 4–4, but I will use utility instead of dollars on this tree. I will substitute utiles, as inferred from the utility function in Figure 4–3, for each of the dollar amounts on your terminal branches in Figure 4–2. Next, using all the probabilities from Figure 4–2, I will fold the tree back by calculating expected utilities. The procedure for doing this is exactly the same as for calculating expected dollars. The difference is that I am calculating something that is to be interpreted as expected personal dollars rather than expected objective dollars, and the final result is displayed in Figure 4–4.

BROKER: But what does this result mean?

ANALYST: I will need to draw one other tree, in Figure 4–5, to show you what it means. You will recall that a certainty equivalent is approximately the same as the expected value minus the risk premium.

BROKER: Right.

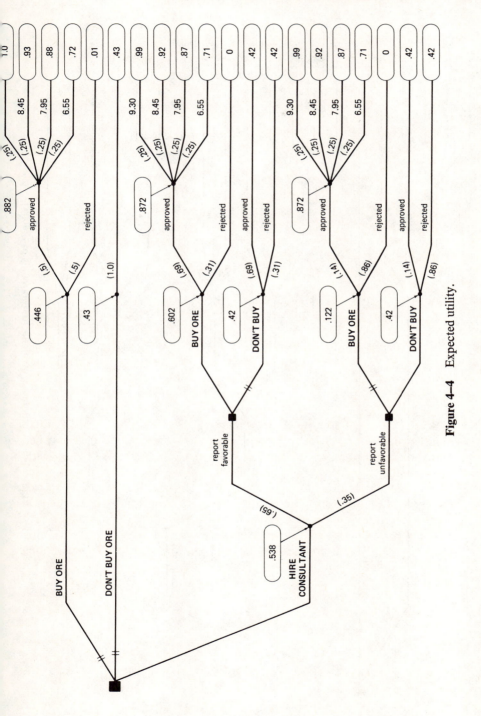

Figure 4–4 Expected utility.

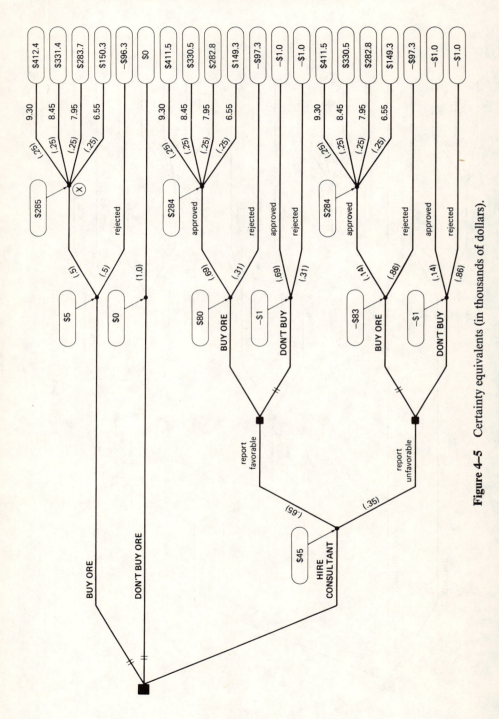

Figure 4–5   Certainty equivalents (in thousands of dollars).

ANALYST: And I told you earlier that I wanted certainty equivalents at all of the nodes in the decision tree?

BROKER: That's right.

ANALYST: Now I can obtain those certainty equivalents simply by using all of the utiles in the decision tree in Figure 4–4 and substituting the dollars indicated by the utility function in Figure 4–3.

BROKER: I'll take your word for that.

ANALYST: No, I would rather have you challenge the point a bit. How do you feel about the selling prices or certainty equivalents in Figure 4–5? Do you wish to argue about any of them? Consider the branch in the upper right hand corner that is labeled X. I have calculated a certainty equivalent of $285,000 whereas you earlier estimated $275,000.

BROKER: That is an interesting discrepancy. Remember when I said that I felt so uncomfortable about the estimate of $275,000? I think that I was pushing that estimate a little lower than it should be because of being so unsure about it. So the calculation of $285,000 does not really seem very unreasonable.

But now let me check the other numbers that you have calculated. [*After considerable examination and hesitation*] The initial certainty equivalent associated with hiring a consultant in Figure 4–5 is so *much* lower than the corresponding expected value in Figure 4–2. The certainty equivalent suggests that this deal is worth $45,000, whereas the expected value shown it as worth over $100,000.

ANALYST: That's right. The big decrease, of course, is a result of your conservative attitude toward risk. Does the size of those initial certainty equivalents in Figure 4–5 make sense to you?

BROKER: They actually seem more reasonable than the expected values. In fact, I feel more comfortable with Figure 4–5 than with Figure 4–2. The certainty equivalents may not be perfect, but they certainly seem to be in the right ball park. In fact, I have a hunch that I am more willing to go along with the values in Figure 4–5 than I would be if I had intuitively estimated all of those certainty equivalents myself.

ANALYST: I agree. It would have been terribly difficult to make all those estimates.

And now, I have some good news for you. This concludes our analysis.

BROKER: That must mean that I should go out and hire a consultant since that initial act has a higher selling price than any of the other acts.

ANALYST: That's the conclusion to be derived from the analysis. Of course, there may be some other factors that we haven't formally considered, but based upon all of your inputs—your probability estimates, your evaluation of nonmonetary criteria, and your attitude toward risk—your best choice seems to be to begin by hiring the consultant.

BROKER: This is where we were about halfway through the analysis, but

I am much more comfortable with that strategy now. I will phone him right away, and I will get in touch with you in about three months to let you know how things turned out.

ASSIGNMENTS

1. The utility curve in Figure 4–3 is based upon the assumption that the broker evaluated the gamble with a 50 percent chance of winning $412,400 and a 50 percent chance of losing $97,300 as being worth a certainty equivalent of $25,000. Assume now that he reevaluates his attitude toward risk and decides that his certainty equivalent is $0. Calculate the implied certainty equivalents of the three initial courses of action specified by the new certainty equivalent of the gamble.

2. Based upon these new calculations, how would you expect the relative values of these three certainty equivalents to vary as the result of a sensitivity analysis that first assumes greater risk aversion and then less risk aversion on the part of the broker?

5

DECISION-TREE EXERCISES

The exercises in this chapter and the Waggoner case in Chapter 6 are intended to develop fluency in turning simple perceptions of a decision problem into a decision tree and critically evaluating the output.

5.1 WIDGETS INC.

Make whatever simplifying assumptions are necessary to obtain a calculable answer to the following exercise:

It was 8:00 P.M. and C. W. Dobbs, a salesman for Widgets Incorporated, was considering whether his planned trip to New York, costing $100, to see the purchasing agent of Nichols and Sons would be a washout. He knew that the agent was only in the city for one week in two. However, if the agent were in the city, Dobbs believed that the chances were 3 to 2 that he could get an order. If he got an order, his commission would be $200.

"I'd give my right arm to know whether I'll get an order on this trip," he grumbled. Then he recalled a service known as Executive Checkoff, which for $8 could inform him whether Nichols' purchasing agent was in New York City. Because of the hour, Dobbs knew that this was the only source of information available to him.

a. Assuming he does not use Executive Checkoff, should Dobbs make the trip?
b. How much does Dobbs value his right arm—that is, what should he be willing to pay for perfect information as to whether the trip would produce an order?
c. Should Dobbs purchase the information from Executive Checkoff? Give your reasons. What has all this to do with buying marketing research?

How would you adjust your analyses of the previous questions if:

d. Dobbs has a "friend" in New York he would be glad of an excuse to visit?
e. He would be in financial difficulties if he lost $100?
f. He does not know for sure what the size of the orders would be and, therefore, the size of his commission?
g. Checkoff may make a mistake about the agent's being in New York?

5.2 NEW ENGLAND RAILROAD COMPANY

In 1963 the New England Railroad Company (NERC) was considering the possibility of adding a new economy class to the two existing classes— first class and tourist—in the hope that the total contribution to its profit from fares might be increased. R. H. Welch, the marketing manager for NERC, had to decide within the next week whether or not to introduce such a change. If introduced, the new class would have to be retained for at least 100 days. Welch felt that the essential question to be answered in his analysis was whether such a deal would attract sufficient new customers to offset the loss of revenue from existing tourist customers switching to the lower-contribution economy class.

Welch, having had some experience with these problems in the past, made the following assessments:

a. On an average day he felt that there was a 1 in 3 chance that 200 new customers would be attracted to the new class, a 1 in 3 chance that the figure would be around 100 new customers, and a 1 in 3 chance that it would be about 50.
b. Similarly, Welch felt there was a 1 in 3 chance that on an average each day 100 people would switch from the existing tourist class to the new economy class, a 1 in 3 chance that there would be about 50 switchers, and a 1 in 3 chance that there would be about 25.
c. The Cost Accounting Department estimated that the tourist fare contributed $10 to overhead and profit and the economy fare about $4.
d. Welch thought that the fixed cost of introducing the new class would be about $5,000.
e. Welch felt that both he and NERC could afford to "play the averages" in making this decision.

Would you, as R. H. Welch, introduce the new fare class? Show your decision tree for the problem, *using change in expected contribution as your criterion*. Make any obvious simplifying assumptions. (This is an exercise, not a realistic case.) You may find it convenient to compute the consequences of any act-event sequence by first noting on the corresponding branches of the tree the effect on contribution of each act and event.

DECISION-TREE CASELET

6.1 WAGGONER ENGINEERING CORPORATION (A)[1]

On August 14, 1969, L. E. Waggoner had only a few more days in which to make up his mind whether or not to sign a proposed contract with a syndicate of businessmen in the city of Norwood. The contract provided that the Waggoner Engineering Corporation, of which Waggoner was president, should build a community television antenna according to certain specifications on a site some distance from the city and link it to a distributing point near the center of the city; the local syndicate would then pay Waggoner in cash for the complete system and take over its operation.

The Waggoner Engineering Corporation's sole business was the design and construction of community antenna systems to service towns and small cities beyond the reach of existing television broadcast facilities. The company had been founded by L. E. Waggoner in 1965, after he had received a master's degree in civil and electrical engineering from Georgia Tech in June 1963 and then spent two years working in the Broadcasting Facilities Department of a major television network. Its initial capital had consisted of $15,000 paid in by Waggoner's father, a successful construction contractor. Since the founding of the company, all of its stock had been held by members of the Waggoner family. The company's assets on August 14, 1969, amounted to $75,000, of which $40,000 represented cash and the remainder represented the net book value of construction and office equipment.

In order to conserve working capital,[2] Waggoner had a firm policy of avoiding involvement in the ownership and operation of any antenna system

---

[1] Modified and reprinted with permission of the President and Fellows of Harvard College. Copyright © 1965 by the President and Fellows of Harvard College.

[2] Working capital, also called net current assets, is defined as equal to net liquid assets plus inventories.

once it had been completed and tested. In developing a new location the company obtained a franchise from the city government and then, before committing any resources to actual construction, tried to interest local businessmen and investors in forming a local company to purchase and operate the system as soon as it was completed and proved out. When Waggoner failed to organize a local group that would contract for purchase of the system on satisfactory terms, he invariably preferred to forfeit the franchise rather than tie up his capital for an indefinite period of time. On August 14, 1969, Waggoner held only one franchise, the one in the city of Norwood, and saw no prospect of getting another one within the next several months. The Norwood franchise would become invalid unless construction "begins not later than September 1 and continues thereafter with no unnecessary or undue delays."

The only suitable location for the antenna at Norwood was at a very substantial distance from the city, and, therefore, it would be more economical to transmit the television signals from the antenna to the distributing point in the center of Norwood by microwave relay than by coaxial cable. Such microwave transmission required a license from the Federal Communications Commission (FCC), however, and because there was a local television station in Norwood, it was not at all certain what action the FCC would take concerning Waggoner's application for a license. The license might be granted without restrictions, but in similar circumstances in the recent past the FCC had sometimes restricted the license to prohibit transmission of programs that the local station wished to rebroadcast by use of kinescope recordings and sometimes refused to grant any license at all. The examiner's report on the Waggoner case was not to be rendered until December 15, and Waggoner knew of no way of getting any advance indication of the examiner's conclusion. He felt sure, however, that the commission would accept the examiner's recommendation in this case whichever way the examiner ruled.

The granting of a restricted license would be disadvantageous to Waggoner because the proposed contract with the Norwood syndicate specified a price of only $120,000 for a system with a microwave connection and a restricted license, whereas it specified a price of $150,000 for a system with a microwave connection and unrestricted license. The syndicate would also pay $150,000 for a system with connection by coaxial cable, over which the FCC would have no control, but whereas construction of the system would cost only about $110,000 if a microwave link were used, it would cost about $180,000 if a cable connection were necessary. Although no money would have to be spent on equipment for either type of connection until after the examiner's report was received on December 15, the terms of the franchise meant that the antenna itself, which accounted for about $80,000 of the total cost, would have to be nearly if not quite completed before that date.

Diagram the decision problem that Waggoner faced on August 14, 1969, and value the end positions of the diagram in the way that you believe would be most helpful to Waggoner. Do not try to decide what Waggoner should do.

6.2   WAGGONER ENGINEERING CORPORATION (B)

On August 15, 1969, before he had made up his mind whether or not to sign the contract with the local group in Norwood that was described in Waggoner Engineering Corporation (A), L. E. Waggoner learned quite unexpectedly that a competitor, the Electronics Service Corporation, was willing to sell him a franchise and contract held by Electronics in the city of Prescott; the price would be $10,000 cash. Waggoner had offered to buy the franchise and contract at that price some months before, but at that time Electronics had flatly refused to sell. Electronics now indicated that they had another offer for the franchise and contract, in the amount of $9,000, which they would accept if Waggoner did not close the deal within one week. Although the Prescott franchise had come along unexpectedly, Waggoner felt quite sure that the chance of his being offered still another franchise within the next several months was virtually nil.

The contract with the local operating group at Prescott called for an antenna to be erected on a hill just outside the city and to be connected by cable with a distributing point in the city. The price to be paid by the group for the completed system was $140,000, and from the investigation he had conducted before making his original offer, Waggoner had concluded that he could build the complete system for about $90,000, provided that he could get by with an antenna 100 feet high, as he hoped he could. There was some risk, however, that an antenna only 100 feet high would not receive a signal of the strength and clarity required by the contract, since a mountain range partially obstructed the antenna's reception. If the 100-foot antenna did prove insufficient, Waggoner was certain he could increase its height to a point where the signal was not obstructed for an additional cost of $70,000; virtually none of this extra cost could be saved by building the higher antenna to begin with.

The local group and the city government had agreed to allow Electronics to sell the franchise and contract to Waggoner. The franchise was valid provided that the system was in operation on April 1, 1970, and Waggoner felt absolutely sure that construction would take less than three months, even if he had to work on the Norwood job at the same time and even if the height of the antenna at Prescott had to be increased. Waggoner would, however, have to deposit $5,000 with the operating group within one week of taking over the contract, and he would have to agree that if he should fail to complete the system, the deposit would be forfeited in lieu of any suit the operating group might have brought.

Diagram the decision problem that Waggoner faced on August 15, 1969, and value the end positions of the diagram in the way that you believe would be most helpful to Waggoner. Do not try to decide what Waggoner should do.

6.3   WAGGONER ENGINEERING CORPORATION (C)

On August 16, 1969, Waggoner decided to make a systematic analysis of the decision problem that he faced regarding the proposed contract with a syndicate of local businessmen in the city of Norwood and the offer that he had received from the Electronics Service Corporation. He assessed the following probabilities:

License for Microwave Connection at Norwood

Granted without restrictions	.5
Granted with restrictions	.2
Refused	.3
	1.0

Increase in Height of Antenna at Prescott

Necessary	.3
Unnecessary	.7
	1.0

Assuming that Mr. Waggoner is willing to treat expected values as certainty equivalents in analyzing his decision problem:

1. Determine Waggoner's optimal strategy and his certainty-equivalent value for that strategy.
2. Determine Waggoner's certainty-equivalent values for each of the following strategies:
   a. Accept and complete both Norwood and Prescott.
   b. Accept Norwood, but refuse Prescott.
   c. Refuse Norwood, but accept and complete Prescott.
3. Using your answers to problem 2, compute Waggoner's certainty equivalent for the uncertain total cash flow that will result from each of the three strategies defined there. Then compare your result for strategy (a) with the sum of your results for strategies (b) and (c).

6.4   WAGGONER ENGINEERING CORPORATION (D)

After thinking more carefully about the possible consequences of his possible courses of action, Waggoner decided that his certainty equivalents for some of the gambles he might face would not be at all close to his corresponding expected values. After some further thought, he decided to base his analysis on his preferences for net liquid assets on April 1, 1970. Selecting +$150,000, −$20,000 as the high and low asset values, he assessed a utility curve, of which two portions are shown in Figure 6–1. Assuming that none of the acts or events in the decision problem he was facing would in any way alter his nonmonetary assets:

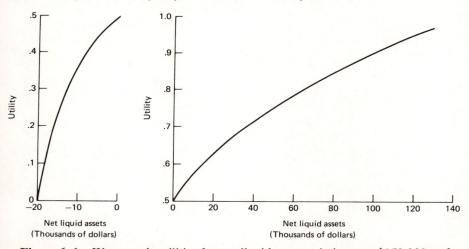

Figure 6–1   Waggoner's utilities for net liquid assets relative to +$150,000 and −$20,000.

1.   Determine Waggoner's optimal strategy and his certainty-equivalent value for that strategy.
2.   Determine Waggoner's certainty-equivalent values for each of the following strategies:
     a.   Accept and complete both Norwood and Prescott.
     b.   Accept Norwood, but refuse Prescott.
     c.   Refuse Norwood, but accept and complete Prescott.
3.   Using your answers to 2, compute Waggoner's certainty equivalent for the uncertain total cash flow that will result from each of the three strategies defined above, and then compare your results for strategies (b) and (c). Does your result for (a) equal the sum of your results for (b) and (c)?
4.   Compute Waggoner's certainty equivalents for even chances at each of the following pairs of values of his criterion and be prepared to discuss what

your certainty equivalents for these gambles would be if you were in Waggoner's position.

a.   −$20,000 and $0
b. $0 and +$20,000
c. $0 and +$50,000
d.   +$50,000 and +$100,000

$$ $$

7

DECISION ANALYSIS IN USE[1]

7.1 ACTUAL AND POTENTIAL IMPACT ON MANAGEMENT

The body of techniques that we refer to as decision analysis has begun to play a major role in business management since the 1960s. As might be expected when a radically new approach is used, business executives have, on occasion, found these methods frustrating and unrewarding. Nevertheless, there seems to be a steadily growing conviction in the management community that decision analysis should, and will, occupy an important place in an executive's arsenal of problem-solving techniques. There is even some indication that it is fast dominating "management science" as an operational tool.

The use of decision analysis is not restricted only to investment, marketing, or other types of business decisions. Potential and actual applications are also to be found in the areas of medicine, the military, engineering, and government.

Many companies are using decision analysis and we anticipate that its use will increase at an ever-increasing rate. This forecast is based not only on partisan judgment that it is a powerful tool, but also on the fact that thousands of recipients of Masters degrees in Business Administration (MBA) who are trained in decision analysis are entering the business world each year and the number of senior managers familiar with decision analysis is rapidly expanding. Robert Newman, former manager of Planning Services at General Electric, has forecast that:

> Within ten years, decision theory, conversational computers, and library programs should occupy the same role for the manager as calculus, slide rules, and mathematical tables do for the engineer today. The engineer of Roman

[1] Based partly on an article by Rex V. Brown, "Do Managers Find Decision Theory Useful?" *Harvard Business Review* (May–June 1970), pp. 78–89.

times had none of these, but he could make perfectly good bridges. However, he could not compete today even in bridge building, let alone astroengineering. Management is today at the stage of Roman engineering. Needless to say, managers will still use specialists, just as engineers use heat transfer experts.

Newman's time schedule may be overly optimistic, but we are in broad agreement with the substance of his view.

The following examples of current uses, culled largely from a 1969–1970 survey[2] of decision analysis in use in twenty organizations, are intended to give an appreciation of the current state of the art and an introductory feeling for what it is like to be a manager who uses decision analysis.

Executives and staff specialists in the companies surveyed provided the bulk of the material. The survey included three organizations with several years of active experience with decision analysis (E. I. Du Pont de Nemours & Company, The Pillsbury Company, and the General Electric Company); a sampling of corporations that had begun to use it two or three years before the survey and were quite actively employing it at the time of the survey (for example, General Mills, Incorporated and Inmont Corporation); two organizations whose experience had been disappointing; a few companies (such as Ford Motor Company and Time, Incorporated) with a definite interest in decision analysis but—at least, as of 1969—few applications; and a few consulting firms with well-known expertise in the area (notably Arthur D. Little, Incorporated, and McKinsey & Company).

During the course of the survey particular attention was focused on the following questions:

What tangible impact does decision analysis have on how businesses are run and on how individual decisions are made?

What areas of decision making is decision analysis best suited for?

What practical benefits result?

What trends in usage are apparent?

What obstacles and pitfalls lie in the way of more effective usage?

What organization steps should management take to use decision analysis more effectively?

What remains to be done in developing and expanding the usefulness of decision analysis?

7.2   GROWING USE

Only a few United States companies have used decision analysis in their operations for a significant period of time. Du Pont initiated it in the late

2 Performed by one of the authors for the Marketing Science Institute of Cambridge, Mass.

1950s and Pillsbury in the early 1960s. However, since the mid-1960s there has been a dramatic increase in this activity. Executive interest was aroused by articles in the *Harvard Business Review,* executive orientation seminars, reports of successful applications by pioneering companies, and perhaps most important of all, a steady stream of trained MBAs entering managerial ranks in substantial numbers. The principal intellectual thrust behind most of these developments was the technical work and teaching of Robert O. Schlaifer and Howard Raiffa at the Harvard Business School.[3]

Stimulated by these developments, executives in a number of companies began to explore the potential applications of decision analysis to their own operations. For example, General Electric set up an intensive study by a high-level committee that led to major changes in plant appropriation methods. Ford Motor and other companies put literally hundreds of their middle and senior managers through training programs varying in length from a few days to several weeks, and other companies, including General Mills, began to introduce decision analysis on a project basis.

7.3 IMPACT ON DECISION MAKING

Since the companies in the survey were selected on the basis of their actual or imputed use of decision analysis, no special significance can be attached to the fact that most of them do indeed use the tools. In reality, in fact, even these companies do not show drastic changes in their general decision-making procedures because of exposure to decision analysis. This we attribute largely to the fact that senior decision makers have not yet been trained to incorporate the new technology into their personal decision processes. Indeed, the applications we have uncovered have been largely carried out by specialist decision analysts and have not been (with some worthwhile exceptions) under the informed control of the manager himself. We believe that the turning point will come when substantial numbers of managers can incorporate decision analysis naturally into their everyday thinking.

Nevertheless, individual decisions of managers have often been profoundly affected by their exposure to decision analysis. Examples from the experience of the most active companies interviewed—Du Pont, Pillsbury, General Electric, and Ford—give some measure of how decision analysis is being used by managers.

---

[3] See, for example, Robert O. Schlaifer, *Analysis of Decisions Under Uncertainty* (New York: McGraw-Hill, 1969), and Howard Raiffa, *Decision Analysis* (Reading, Mass.: Addison-Wesley, 1968).

7.3.1   E. I. Du Pont de Nemours & Company

Substantial decision-analysis activity occurs throughout the Du Pont organization, stimulated by staff groups in the Development Department and elsewhere. Managers in the various departments have shown increasing interest in the staff groups' services, which are supplied for a fee.

J. T. Axon, manager of the Management Sciences Division, commented during the survey that his decision analysts "have indeed been pioneers and missionaries on behalf of decision analysis within Du Pont, and I share with them the conviction that their work has improved the quality of numerous decisions around the company. Their impact has been seriously limited, however, by the absence of appropriate educational efforts aimed at the decision makers. Even at this date, we have in Du Pont, in my judgment, very few key decision makers who are 'alive' to its possibilities and comfortable in its use. It is this lack that has dragged down the Du Pont effort."

At Du Pont middle and even senior managers increasingly take actions or submit recommendations that have decision analysis along with more conventional analyses as their base, but the presentation to top management is likely to be supported by more informal reasoning.

In the case of a new product that had just reached the prototype stage at Du Pont, for example, the question before management was, on what scale should initial pilot production be carried out? Critical uncertainties involved the reliability of the military demand for which the prototype had been originally designed and the amount of supplementary commercial business that would be generated. Decision analysis was performed on a computer to produce "value distributions" of return on investment for various plant sizes and pricing strategies. The inputs to the analysis included probability assessments of demand for each possible end use of the product (based on market research) as well as assessments of production cost and timing. On the basis of the assessments used, the analysis indicated that a certain price was optimal and that a $3 million pilot plant would have the highest expected rate of return. When this conclusion was transmitted to top management, it was couched in the language of informal reasoning. Management adopted, unchanged, the pricing recommendation of the study, but it opted for a smaller, $1 million plant. Apparently top management was risk-averse, contrary to assumptions of the analysis.

One of the first lessons of decision analysis in use is illustrated here. While such analysis can, in principle, address any decision problem with unimpeachable rigor, the conclusions are only as good as the inputs. It is by no means a trivial task to ensure that the problem you solve is the *problem you have.*

7.3.2   The Pillsbury Company

James R. Petersen, vice president of The Pillsbury Company and general manager of its Grocery Products Company at the time of the survey, used decision trees regularly in evaluating major recommendations submitted to him. He approved more than a dozen marketing decisions a year on the basis of the findings of detailed decision analysis. (Many more decisions in his divisions were rendered after first using a skeletal decision tree to clarify the key problem issues.) Typically, a middle manager in the Grocery Products Company spent a week or so developing an approach using decision analysis, often with the help of a staff specialist. When the middle manager's recommendation was considered by Petersen, this analysis was the vehicle for the discussion of his proposal.

In one instance the issue before management was whether to switch from a box to a bag as a package for a certain grocery product.[4] Petersen and his sales manager had been disposed to retain the box on the grounds of greater customer appeal. The brand manager, however, favored the bag on cost grounds. He supported his recommendation with a decision analysis based on his own best assessments of probable economic, marketing, and other consequences. When despite the sales manager's more pessimistic assessments of the market impact the bag still looked more profitable, Petersen adopted the brand manager's recommendation. The bag was introduced, and the profits on the product climbed substantially.

During discussions some Pillsbury executives urged that the bag be test marketed before management made a firm decision. The original decision analysis showed, however, only a chance of 1 in 10 that the bag would prove unprofitable, and if that occurred, it would probably be not too unprofitable. A simple supplementary analysis demonstrated that the value of making a market test could not remotely approach its cost. Accordingly, no test marketing was undertaken. Management's confidence in the analysis was later confirmed by the bag's success.

7.3.3   General Electric Company

About 1966 General Electric (GE) ordered that all investment requests of more than $500,000 be supported by a probabilistic assessment of the rate of return and other key measures. More than 500 instances of computerized decision analysis were then conducted over the next four years, largely in the area of plant appropriations.

A library of special decision analysis programs had been developed at GE

---

[4] The talk by Gerald Eskin in Chapter 8 amplifies this example.

largely by Robert Newman, former manager of Planning Services. Managers in other GE operations consult Newman frequently when confronted with a major problem. The consulting relationship, no doubt enhanced by Newman's own experience in line management, often has an impact on issues beyond the scope of the originating inquiry, as the following example shows.

One GE division, faced with a shortage of manufacturing capacity for a mature industrial product called on Newman for his evaluation. Using the information and assessments supplied by the division manager, including a suspicion that the product was obsolescent, Newman spent a few hours on a decision analysis and concluded that the division should not increase capacity, but raise prices. Both the consultant and the division manager felt uneasy about this conclusion.

Further discussion yielded new confidential information that the division was developing a product that promised to supplant the old one. This information, plus various estimates of the probability of success and related matters, led to a decision analysis which employed GE's prepackaged computer programs. The analysis indicated that research and development expenditures on the new product should be increased by a factor of 20. The recommendation was adopted. The new product went into production two years later, and it achieved highly-profitable sales of approximately $20 million a year.

7.3.4   Ford Motor Company

Some attempts at decision analysis have yielded discouraging results—at least, initially. At Ford Motor Company about 200 senior executives were given a brief program emphasizing decision analysis during the five-year period 1964–69. Although the program was followed up in some divisions by intensive workshops for junior executives, use of decision analysis at Ford by 1969 had been negligible in the marketing area and the prospects were judged unpromising at least at that time. In the opinion of a key marketing executive, large organizations with diffuse decision-making processes (like Ford) are not as well suited to its effective use as are the small or one-man organizations.

John J. Nevin, vice president of marketing for Ford in 1969, added the following observations:

> I am not sure that there is any reason to be discouraged by the fact that in many other companies decision analysis may be far more accepted and far more utilized by middle management. Maybe all analytical tools sneak into general usage through the back door. It does not seem to me to be improbable that the middle management people, who are more comfortable with these techniques and are using them on very specific technical problems today,

will, as they grow to top management positions, feel as uncomfortable switching to some new decision-making process as many of today's managers feel in switching to a more disciplined analysis.

He also noted that the average executive has difficulty picking up all of the variables in a complex decision-making problem. He attributes this in large part to the executive's inability to discipline himself to use a new technique.

Nevertheless, several Ford divisions subsequently began exploring decision analysis applications at their most senior executive levels, and there have been some instances of very successful implementation. For example, at the Ford Tractor Division a product policy decision was required in a regional market suffering from competitive inroads. The main options were to reduce prices or to introduce one of several possible new models. A modest decision analysis was carried out on these choices. Several runs incorporating assessments and modifications advanced by the marketing manager, the assistant general manager, and the general manager were made. The somewhat controversial conclusion to introduce a certain model was presented to the general manager, who adopted it and initiated the necessary engineering studies.[5]

7.4   HOW DECISION ANALYSIS IS INTEGRATED INTO ORGANIZATIONS

The 1969–1970 survey of decision-analysis use in twenty organizations revealed that it is the organizational arrangements for offering decision analysis that most strongly separate the more from the less successful experiences. The most successful arrangement seems to employ the "vest-pocket" approach, where the analyst works intimately with the executive and typically reports directly to him. Pillsbury's Grocery Products Company and Inmont Corporation are excellent examples of this approach.

At the other end of the spectrum is the "arms-length" approach, which is characteristic of much traditional operations research. In this approach the analysis is performed by a group that is organizationally distant from the executive being served. In such instances the executive may feel threatened rather than supported by decision analysis, and critical weaknesses may consequently develop in the communication of the problem and its analysis.

A common obstacle to the widespread use of decision analysis in companies is a negative attitude toward the usefulness of *attempting* to quantify

---

[5] For a more detailed discussion see "Ford Tractor Division: A Case Study in Product Policy," PDA Working Paper Series, Marketing Science Institute, Cambridge, Mass. (1974).

an uncertainty when the information about the uncertain quantity is weak. This amounts to a rejection of two basic tenets of decision analysis—that subjective judgment, however tenuous, must be taken into account somehow by the decision maker and that a formal approach may do the job more effectively than unaided intuition.

Increase in the effectiveness of decision analysis is to some extent dependent on the state of the art. The development and propagation of economical and quick routines utilizing inputs and outputs that can be readily communicated will no doubt be a major help. Such routines affect the practicality and appeal of decision analysis in a management setting. However, it seems clear that purely theoretical developments are not holding up its further application; the frontiers of the technology are way ahead of the applications, in most cases.

7.5   USE OF CONSULTANTS

The epitome of the arms-length organizational arrangement, which we have found generally less effective than the vest-pocket arrangement, appears in the role of the outside consultant. Our survey suggests that with a few exceptions, to be discussed below, consulting firms are doing relatively little decision-analysis work for their clients. This is significant because potentially consulting firms are a major resource for companies that want to use decision analysis. In addition, leading consultants have done much to explain it to businessmen.[6]

7.5.1   Deterrents to the Use of Consultants

It seems that clients often insist on holding back pertinent data affecting the issue from the consultant—and effective decision analysis depends critically on incorporating in the analysis *all* of the elements that the decision maker sees as important. Many clients prefer to limit consultants to performing clearly specified technical or data-gathering tasks with a minimum of two-way communication; executives worry about jeopardizing company security and giving the consultant too much say in their business.

Harlan Meal, a departmental manager for the consulting firm of Arthur D. Little, makes a telling observation concerning the role of consultants and general obstacles to the adoption of decision analysis:

[6] See, for example, David B. Hertz, "Risk Analysis in Capital Investment," *Harvard Business Review* (January–February 1964), p. 95; and John Magee, "Decision Trees for Decision Making," *Harvard Business Review* (July–August 1964), p. 126, and "How to Use Decision Trees in Capital Investment," *Harvard Business Review* (September–October 1964), p. 79.

Many of the executives who hire consultants or who employ expert technical staff do so in order to reduce the uncertainty in their decision making rather than to improve their ability to deal with uncertain situations. Many of the clients we have want to buy from us information that will make the outcome of a particular course of action more certain than it would otherwise have been. If all we can do for them is reduce the chance of making an incorrect decision or improve the expected performance of the decision they do make in the face of uncertainty, they are not very interested.

It is on this point that I think the application of decision-theory analysis gets stuck nearly every time. Very few executives think of themselves as gamblers or of making the best kind of decisions in a gambling situation. They want, instead, to think of themselves as individuals whose greater grasp of the available information and whose greater insight remove the uncertainty from the situation.

When the information quality is so poor that the assignment of probabilities to outcomes seems an exercise in futility, decision-theory analysis can be most useful. Yet most executives in such a situation say that the only thing that really can be useful is their own experienced intuition. The executive is going to behave as though he has information about the situation, whether he has it or not.

7.5.2   The Decision Analysis Group at Stanford Research Institute

At the time of this writing consulting in the field of decision analysis is associated largely with two organizations—the Decision Analysis Group at Stanford Research Institute (SRI) in Menlo Park, California, and Decisions and Designs, Incorporated, of McLean, Virginia.[7]

The SRI group, which was the pioneer in the field, grew out of activity initiated by Ronald A. Howard of the Engineering Economic Systems Group at Stanford University.

The SRI group's effort is divided among direct consulting projects, training executives and professionals, and advancing the state of the art—for example, through general-purpose computer programs. Consulting projects undertaken include whether the Federal government should "seed" hurricanes in an attempt to mitigate their impact, the advisability of capital investment in nuclear plants in Mexico, a new-product decision involving $20 million of development cost, and development of ongoing decision-making systems in a corporation.

The main thrust of the group's effort is in projects that require at least

---

[7] Further information on these two organizations can be obtained from the Director, Decision Analysis Group, Stanford Research Institute, Menlo Park, California 94025 and from R. A. Eidson, President, Decisions and Designs, Inc., Suite 600, 7900 Westpark Drive, McLean, Virginia 22101.

three months of work and often as much as several years and in projects where the bulk of their involvement is in constructing models of the problem.

7.5.3 Decisions and Designs, Inc.

Decisions and Designs, Incorporated (DDI), founded in 1971, includes on its staff people with extensive experience in management as well as in decision analysis.

Many of DDI's projects have been related to foreign policy and defense. For example, what is the impact of alternative United States policies on the probability that a particular treaty will be signed during this year? Should economic sanctions be applied to states that fail to enact specific legislation on highway safety? Should a business corporation close down a division? Which contractor should be selected to build a particular technical system for the United States Navy? Which foreign policy in the Mideast will do most to protect energy sources and other United States interests?

Major emphasis has been on structuring the decision-making processes of individual decision makers or advisers rather than constructing large-scale models. Individual projects, therefore, tend to be smaller than those of the SRI group and involve a higher proportion of client contact time.

Other consulting operations active in decision analysis include Applied Systems, Incorporated, of Cambridge, Massachusetts, and McKinsey & Company, of New York City.

7.6 REALIZING THE POTENTIALS

How beneficial is decision analysis to a company? Does it lead to "better" decisions than other approaches to decision making? Logic alone cannot give us the answer. However, it seems clear that two major requirements must be met:

1. The subjective inputs required for the analysis must be accurately measured and recorded. (Executives, as Meal suggests in the comment quoted earlier, may not explicitly admit to uncertainty about some critical variable, whereas they may consider it in their informal reasoning.)
2. The decision analysis should incorporate all the considerations that the executive would informally take into account—for example, some non-monetary side effect, like goodwill. (Where there is good communication between executive and analyst, the executive often can and does make on-the-spot adjustments for anything that has been left out of the analysis. Sometimes, though, such adjustments are so substantial that they swamp and thereby invalidate the entire analysis.)

Consideration of *all* the angles and factors that bear on a good decision analysis (or any other analysis) is time consuming and sometimes quite frustrating. Clearly, though, it is one of the prerequisites to using this approach. The following experience should suffice to make the point:

A corporate staff team at General Mills evaluated an acquisition opportunity by means of a decision analysis computer program that took four months to develop and another two months to run with successively modified inputs corresponding to new assessments and assumptions made by the researchers and executives. In all, 150 computer runs were made before arriving at a recommendation to make the acquisition and to adopt a specific marketing and production strategy. The recommendation was rejected by top management, however, when the company's legal counsel advised against the acquisition on certain legal grounds. The lawyers discovered that a critical consideration had been omitted from the analysis that rendered it unusable for the purpose at hand.

It should be noted that this was the company's first major attempt at applying decision analysis. The experience did perform a valuable function in exposing line and staff to its scope and pitfalls. The company's record since then has been quite successful.

7.7 COST VS. BENEFITS

The costs of applying decision analysis are by no means inconsequential. It is true that the out-of-pocket costs for technicians and computers, even for a large-scale analysis, may be relatively trivial. Moreover, these costs can be expected to decline as decision technology becomes more streamlined.

Other, less obvious costs, however, are not trivial and are unlikely to become so. Critical decisions may be unacceptably delayed while an analysis is being completed. (When General Mills does not use decision analysis for market planning decisions, this is cited as the most common reason.) A busy executive needs to devote some of his valuable time to making sure that all of the relevant judgments he can make have been fed into the analysis.

Even more serious a "cost" may be the discomfort an executive feels as he forces his traditional way of thinking into an unfamiliar mold and lays bare to the discretion of a staff specialist the most delicate considerations that enter into his decision making. These considerations sometimes include confidential information (as in our GE new-product example), admissions of uncertainty, which often run counter to the prevailing managerial culture, and embarrassing motivations. In one instance of an elaborate analysis of possible locations for a European subsidiary, the actual decision was dominated by the fact that key personnel wanted to be near the International

School in Geneva. Somehow, that consideration seemed too noneconomic and nonrational to be fed into the analysis.

However, such costs are by no means prohibitive if management's approach to decision analysis is sound and thorough. When that is the case, the advantages claimed by users of decision analysis are material and persuasive:

1. It focuses informal thinking on the critical elements of a decision.
2. It forces into the open hidden assumptions behind a decision and makes clear their logical implications.
3. It provides an effective vehicle for communicating the reasoning that underlies a recommendation.

Many of the executives most satisfied with decision analysis value it as a vehicle for communicating decision-making reasoning as well as for improving it. Our own feeling is that its contribution to the quality of decision making often seems to come more from forcing meaningful structure on informal reasoning than from supplementing it by formal analysis.

In the Pillsbury Grocery Products Company, for every decision analysis pushed to its numerical conclusion, there are half a dozen cases where only a conceptual decision tree has been drawn. Such a tree is used to focus attention on the critical options and uncertainties and is then dropped in favor of informal reasoning.

7.8 LEARNING THE CRAFT OF DECISION ANALYSIS

The elements of decision analysis as propounded thus far are deceptively simple. You display all relevant acts and events in tree form, attach the probabilities and values (or utilities) in the appropriate places, and then fold the tree back routinely to find the initial decision with the highest expected utility. Many managers and analysts after a little exposure to decision-tree mechanics at the level of Chapters 2 through 4 have felt emboldened to try decision analysis themselves. They have gotten hopelessly entangled or come up with demonstrably ridiculous conclusions and then decided that "decision analysis does not work." It is almost as if we explained to a musical novice the meaning of musical notation and how the keys on the piano work and expected him to play Beethoven's *Moonlight Sonata!*

Perhaps a better analogy would be the schoolboy, who, having mastered a popular article on aeronautics, expects to be able to design a rocket that will go to the moon. While it is true that rocket technology consists, *in principle,* of straightforward extensions of elementary physics, arithmetic, and so forth, a highly trained mind is needed to exploit the potentialities of those extensions. Even when the advanced theory of rocket design has been mastered, a great gulf of engineering implementation has to be bridged before a lunar expedition can be attempted with confidence. The analogy with decision analysis is not so far-fetched. The main difference lies in the fact that no one is likely to *believe* that a short course will equip one to design a rocket. However, he may believe that a short course on decision trees can turn him into a decision analyst.

ASSIGNMENTS

1. It has been argued that any decision can be analyzed using the techniques of decision analysis. Since decision analysis is based on an inescapable logic, an executive should always use it if he wants to make his decisions right. Do you agree? Give your reasons.

2. The basic ideas and technology of decision analysis have been available for well over a decade. Why do you suppose so few companies as yet use it as an integral part of their decision-making process?

3. In what direction will applications of decision analysis expand most rapidly and fruitfully? Consider factors such as industry characteristics (basis of competition, pace of technological change, "progressiveness" of management, profitability); company size and position in industry; decision types (long- versus short-run repetitive versus unique, development, capital investment, pricing, and so forth); and management level or amounts at stake in the decisions.

8

A CASE STUDY IN THE APPLICATION OF DECISION ANALYSIS[1]

8.1 A PACKAGING PROBLEM

One day a product manager of the company with which I was connected said to me, "Gerry, I've got a problem. I've got a product that's packaged in a very expensive container in one particular area of the country and the margins are killing me. I've just got to get out of this thing. I can't afford it. I've been losing money on the product for more than a year." This package was a box type of container; the product was packaged in a bag throughout the rest of the country and the box was substantially more expensive than the bag.

My reaction to this was, "Well, go ahead and use the bag." He answered, "The sales force tells me that I'm likely to lose substantial sales if I were to change the packaging of the product and I'm worried about that, too. But I've got to do it anyway." After I questioned him for a little while, he admitted that he did have the option of not making the change; in fact he did have a decision problem, not just a problem in persuasion.

The product manager suggested that I should work with the sales manager, who was the one complaining about possible sales loss, and that the sales manager and I should put together an analysis and bring it back to him. I then asked the product manager, "If we put together an analysis and it shows that you shouldn't make this change, would you be willing to abide by the results of our analysis?" The answer came back that, no, he would not; he would make the final decision. We then agreed that if he were to make the decision, the analysis would need his inputs. At a later stage the

[1] Transcript of a talk delivered by Dr. Eskin (previously on the staff of The Pillsbury Company) to a seminar for the Marketing Science Institute in Cambridge, Massachusetts, May 1970. Used by permission.

sales force people and the head of the division would be brought in to see if they concurred with our particular reasoning.

There were really two concerns. The first was that if a change in the packaging were made, old customers would not be able to identify the product at first. Then there was a possibility that the change would also create long-run losses in sales because the box was the preferable container.

We decided to break down the problem into two component parts. First, we would look at possible sales loss in the short run due to the identification problem. Second, we would try to determine whether we could recoup any of the early sales losses on the grounds that eventually people would return to the product in spite of the different package.

We assumed it would take about four months to feel the initial effects of sales losses due to the problem of identification. There was no hope that the new package would improve sales. The only question was, By how much would the change in package reduce sales? So the problem was defined in terms of percent loss in sales. Would there be losses in the neighborhood of 10 percent or 20 percent, or what?

The second question was, What would happen in the long run? The long run in this particular case was defined as being fairly short, only another four months, because it was felt that although sales might fall, they should recover fairly rapidly—if they were to recover at all. It was also felt that the best that could happen was that by the end of eight months the original sales figure would be recouped. The worst that could possibly happen was that sales would not recover at all. We also considered the possibility that there would be partial recovery. The alternatives considered are shown in Figure 8–1.

8.2 GETTING PROBABILITY ESTIMATES

Next, we tried to build up a table of betting odds. The first reaction we got was, "I don't know how to put the numbers in a table like that. I don't think sales are going to fall very much, but they are going to fall some." The problem was how do you express this answer in terms of a probability statement.

In this particular case we couldn't get started. Finally, I resorted to picking out numbers for the product manager to react to. I said, "I think the probability of the sales loss being above 20 percent is equal to 50 percent, do you agree?" The answer was "No," and an alternative was supplied by the product manager. And then we finally started moving. (I think that the one sure way to get managers to start specifying in terms of probability statements is to suggest an alternative. Then they will come up

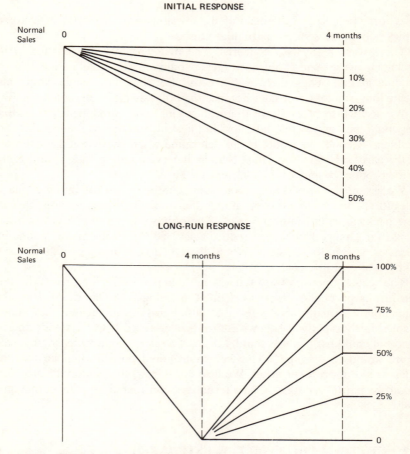

Figure 8–1   Response to change in packaging.

with better estimates, and these can be further refined and tested for consistency.)

In this case the product manager eventually said that he thought there was a 10 percent chance that there would be no sales loss (in the short term), a 45 percent chance that there'd be a 10 percent loss, and so forth as is shown in Table 8–1A. Essentially, he was saying that initially he expected about a 10 percent loss, maybe a little less, but he also saw some possibility of there being an even greater sales loss than that.

The next problem was to assess the chances of long-run recovery. This particular product manager said that if there were large initial sales losses, he thought it was less likely that sales would return to their original level than if initial sales losses were small. We built our probability table around this idea as is shown in Table 8–1B.

Table 8–1   Probabilities Assessed for Effects of Packaging Change on Sales

(A)
Initial Response (4 Months)

Sales Loss	Probability
0	.10
10%	.45
20%	.20
30%	.14
40%	.08
50%	.03

(B)
Long-Run Readjustment

Original Loss	Probability				
	0	25%	50%	75%	100%
0					1.00
10%				.10	.90
20%			.10	.80	.10
30%		.05	.20	.70	.05
40%	.05	.10	.40	.40	.05
50%	.10	.15	.50	.25	0

Given these assumptions and some cost information, we could then calculate the expected value of the bag versus the expected value of the box. Roughly, the expectation was that the sales loss from going to the bag would be about 4 percent over the first year. This was a little surprising in that originally the product manager had been thinking about larger sales losses. However, in his early thinking he had not considered adequately the difference between short-run losses and long-run recovery, nor the fact that the long-run situation was an important part of the assessment. Our analysis indicated that the expected profits resulting from the use of the cheaper bag would be about 10 percent higher than staying with the box. The product manager thereupon decided he should recommend to the general manager of the division that the box be dropped and that the bag be introduced.

8.3   PRESENTING RESULTS TO MANAGEMENT

The proposal was then taken to top management for review. The first reaction received was, "I don't believe your analysis. You know and I know that you can't make a change like that and only observe a 4 percent sales loss." The question then was raised, "What part of the analysis don't you believe?" The answer came back, "I don't believe the conclusion." The follow-up to that remark is, "If you don't believe the conclusion, tell me what part you are questioning in the analysis. Where did we go wrong?" After some discussion, it was agreed that the problem had been properly structured but that the estimates of probability might be in error.

The general manager of the division then went through the process of stating his own estimates of the probabilities; the director of sales also made a set of estimates. Each of these distributions were then put in the model and each one produced a different sales estimate, but the conclusion was the same—changing to the bag would mean higher profits.

At this point some serious interest in the decision modeling approach developed, and it was acknowledged that the analysis might be used for a possible decision. Several other assignments of probabilities were made. Some attempt was made to look at different assumptions, such as what would happen if the sales continued to fall for eight months rather than four months. A number of sensitivity analyses were made. The results were essentially the same: they all indicated that making a change would be more profitable than keeping the current form.

8.4   DECIDE NOW OR TEST?

This raised a new alternative. The head of the division suggested, "Why do we have to make a decision at this point? Why don't we go out into a test market and we'll find out which of these two alternatives really is best." The director of research declared that he could not market test the entire problem in a short period of time, but he did think he could provide information on the initial sales losses. That is, he could go into the market on a limited basis and try the alternate packages to find out whether there would be initial sales losses; but he did not think he could say anything about the long-run situation.

We had at this point two schools of thought: make the decision right away, or do test marketing first. Out of these two schools developed a third, which suggested putting all the facts in the decision model and asking the model for help in answering the question of the advisability of testing.

It was decided to give the modeling approach another try. We started from the position that if a test were not conducted, the decision would be made to change to the bag since this alternative had the highest profit expectancy. With this premise the only possible benefit to the testing would be that it might show that we had made an incorrect tentative decision; hence it might convince us to change our minds. The value of the test could then be measured in terms of the losses that could be *prevented* by doing the test. This value of testing could then be compared to the cost of testing.

We first calculated the value of *perfect* information, or value of losses that could be prevented by a perfect piece of research.[2] We did not believe that we could actually *do* such research. This was to provide a limit; actual (imperfect) research could be worth *no more than this*. The expected value of the type of research that could actually be done was also calculated.

The value of perfect information turned out to be the most useful calculation in that it showed that the maximum value of even an error-free research project was only $4,000.

In this case there was no way in which the proposed research could be done for this price; hence it was concluded that researching the issue would not be worthwhile.

At this point a decision was made. We agreed not to do any further research. We agreed to tool up for changing. Plates and new packaging material were purchased, and production of the new package was started. But just to be safe, we decided to try the bag container in only one small market for a few months before going on to the rest of the region. If the bag were well received, then we would branch out, but if something adverse showed up in this little submarket, then we would stop and reconsider.

Does this decision imply that the model was not really used? In my opinion, this is an example of a very appropriate use of the model because two new alternatives were generated.

The first new alternative was to market test the venture. That was disposed of by doing a value-of-information analysis, and the decision was made that we should not test in the conventional way, namely, by doing a full-blown market research project, because this would be too expensive an undertaking. The second alternative was to reduce our risk somewhat by first trying out the bag in a limited market.

It is such use of decision models that I personally have found to be most valuable: namely, to *generate new alternatives,* to *test* and *communicate* judgments, to better *understand the nature of a problem,* and to allow tests

---

[2] In essence, the value of perfect information is defined as equal to the "expected loss" associated with making a decision without any information except whatever is reflected in the decision maker's "betting odds" in his original analysis of the problem. Since these odds imply uncertainty about the best course of action to follow, there is an expected loss involved in any decision.

of *sensitivity*. In the case I have been discussing the model was *not* used to make a decision; it was used as an *input* in the decision-making process. This is a creative and productive approach to the use of decision analysis, in which the model and management judgment play complementary roles.

ASSIGNMENT

1. Draw a decision tree for the problem described in section 8.2—the choice between keeping the present box container versus switching to a bag. Carefully label each act and event on your tree.

2. Suppose the company switches to a bag container and sales drop dramatically. In this situation, it would be feasible to at least consider switching back to the original box. Has this possibility been taken into account in the decision-tree model you constructed in response to the previous question? If not, why not? Supposing you, as a top manager, felt that such a possibility would deserve consideration, and that you were presented with an analysis, based on your previous tree, indicating that the switch from box to bag should be made. Would you accept this conclusion? What if such an analysis instead indicated that the switch should not be made: would you accept this conclusion?

3. Draw a decision tree for the decision, described in section 8.4, of whether or not to carry out a market test of the bag. Label all branches carefully, particularly those branches representing the possible outcomes of the market test.

4. The author of this case study suggests that decision analysis was helpful in suggesting new action alternatives for analysis. What alternatives can you suggest for consideration which are not mentioned in the case study? Did you make use of decision analysis in developing these alternatives? If not, how would you describe the process you followed in generating alternatives?

5. Using the data in Table 8–1, determine the probability that the long-run sales loss will exceed 25 percent. Determine the conditional probability that *given* a long-run loss of 10 percent, the short-run loss was also 10 percent. (*Hint:* You will find it helpful to draw a probability diagram.)

BIBLIOGRAPHY

AITCHISON, JOHN. *Choice Against Chance: An Introduction to Statistical Decision Theory.* Reading, Mass.: Addison-Wesley Publishing Company, 1970.

ANTHONY, ROBERT N. *Management Accounting: Text and Cases,* 4th Ed. Homewood, Ill.: Richard D. Irwin, Inc., 1968.

BIERMAN, JR., HAROLD. *Financial Policy Decisions.* New York: The Macmillan Company, 1970.

BIERMAN, JR., HAROLD, CHARLES P. BONINI, and WARREN H. HAUSMAN. *Quantitative Analysis for Business Decisions.* Homewood, Ill.: Richard D. Irwin, Inc., 1973.

BRABB, GEORGE. *Introduction to Quantitative Management.* New York: Holt, Rinehart and Winston, Inc., 1968.

BROWN, REX V. *Research and the Credibility of Estimates.* Homewood, Ill.: Richard D. Irwin, Inc., 1971.

BROWN, REX V., ANDREW S. KAHR, and CAMERON PETERSON. *Decision Analysis for the Manager.* New York: Holt, Rinehart and Winston, Inc., 1974.

CHOU, YA-LUN. *Probability and Statistics for Decision Making.* New York: Holt, Rinehart and Winston, Inc., 1972.

CHURCHMAN, C. WEST. *Prediction and Optimal Decision: Philosophical Issues of a Science of Values.* Englewood Cliffs, N.J.: Prentice-Hall, Inc., 1961.

CRAMÉR, HAROLD. *Elements of Probability Theory and Some of Its Applications.* New York: John Wiley & Sons, Inc., 1955.

EDWARDS, WARD and AMOS TVERSKY, ed. *Decision Making: Selected Readings.* Harmondsworth, England: Penguin Books, Ltd., 1967.

FELLER, WILLIAM. *Introduction to Probability Theory and Its Applications,* 2nd Ed. 2 vols. New York: John Wiley & Sons, Inc., 1966 and 1971.

FELLNER, WILLIAM. *Probability and Profit.* Homewood, Ill.: Richard D. Irwin, Inc., 1965.

FISHBURN, PETER C. *Decision and Value Theory.* New York: John Wiley & Sons, Inc., 1964.

FORESTER, JOHN. *Statistical Selection of Business Strategies*. Homewood, Ill.: Richard D. Irwin, Inc., 1968.

GRAYSON, JR., C. JACKSON. *Decisions Under Uncertainty: Drilling Decisions by Oil and Gas Operators*. Boston, Mass.: Harvard Business School Division of Research, 1960.

GREEN, PAUL E. and DONALD S. TULL. *Research for Marketing Decisions*, 2nd Ed. Englewood Cliffs, N.J.: Prentice-Hall, Inc., 1970.

GUENTHER, WILLIAM C. *Concepts of Probability*. New York: McGraw-Hill Book Company, Inc., 1968.

HALEY, CHARLES W. and LAWRENCE D. SCHALL. *The Theory of Financial Decisions*. New York: McGraw-Hill Book Company, Inc., 1973.

HARVARD BUSINESS REVIEW. *Statistical Decision Series* (Parts I–IV). Boston, Mass.: 1951–70.

HAYS, W. L. and R. L. WINKLER. *Statistics: Probability, Inference and Decision*. 2 vols. New York: Holt, Rinehart and Winston, Inc., 1970.

HOROWITZ, IRA. *An Introduction to Quantitative Business Analysis,* 2nd Ed. New York: McGraw-Hill Book Company, Inc., 1972.

HOWARD, RONALD A. *Dynamic Probabilistic Systems*. 2 vols. New York: John Wiley & Sons, Inc., 1971.

JURAN, JOSEPH M. *Managerial Breakthrough: A New Concept of the Manager's Job*. New York: McGraw-Hill Book Company, Inc., 1965.

KEPNER, CHARLES H. and BENJAMIN B. TREGOE. *The Rational Manager*. New York: McGraw-Hill Book Company, Inc., 1965.

KING, WILLIAM R. *Probability for Management Decisions*. New York: John Wiley & Sons, Inc., 1968.

KYBURG, HENRY E. and HOWARD E. SMOKLER, ed. *Studies in Subjective Probability*. New York: John Wiley & Sons, Inc., 1965.

LIFSON, MELVIN W. *Decision and Risk Analysis for Practicing Engineers*. Boston, Mass.: Cahners Books, 1972.

LINDLEY, DENNIS V. *Introduction to Probability and Statistics from a Bayesian Viewpoint*. 2 vols. Cambridge, England: Cambridge University Press, 1965.

MCMILLAN, CLAUDE, and RICHARD F. GONZALEZ. *Systems Analysis—A Computer Approach to Decision Models,* 3rd Ed. Homewood, Ill.: Richard D. Irwin, Inc., 1971.

MILLER, DAVID W. and MARTIN K. STARR. *The Structure of Human Decisions*. Englewood Cliffs, N.J.: Prentice-Hall, Inc., 1967.

MORRIS, WILLIAM T. *The Analysis of Management Decisions,* Rev. Ed. Homewood, Ill.: Richard D. Irwin, Inc., 1964.

MORRIS, WILLIAM T. *The Capacity Decision System.* Homewood, Ill.: Richard D. Irwin, Inc., 1967.

MORRIS, WILLIAM T. *Management Science: A Bayesian Introduction.* Englewood Cliffs, N.J.: Prentice-Hall, Inc., 1968.

NEWMAN, JOSEPH W. *Management Applications of Decision Theory.* New York: Harper & Row Publishers, 1971.

ODIORNE, GEORGE S. *Management Decisions by Objectives.* Englewood Cliffs, N. J.: Prentice-Hall, Inc., 1969.

PESSEMIER, EDGAR A. *New Product Decisions—An Analytic Approach.* New York: McGraw-Hill Book Company, Inc., 1966.

PRATT, JOHN W., HOWARD RAIFFA and ROBERT SCHLAIFER. *Introduction to Statistical Decision Theory.* New York: McGraw-Hill Book Company, Inc., 1965.

RAIFFA, HOWARD and ROBERT SCHLAIFER. *Applied Statistical Decision Theory.* Boston, Mass.: Harvard Business School Division of Research, 1961.

RAIFFA, HOWARD. *Decision Analysis: Introductory Lectures on Choices Under Uncertainty.* Reading, Mass.: Addison-Wesley Publishing Company, 1968.

Risk Analysis—Proceedings of the United States Army Operations Research Symposium, 15–18 May 1972. Washington, D.C.: Office of the Chief of Research and Development, Department of the Army, 1972.

SCHLAIFER, ROBERT. *Probability and Statistics for Business Decisions.* New York: McGraw-Hill Book Company, Inc., 1959.

SCHLAIFER, ROBERT. *Analysis of Decisions Under Uncertainty.* New York: McGraw-Hill Book Company, Inc., 1969.

SCHLAIFER, ROBERT. *Computer Programs for Elementary Decision Analysis.* Boston, Mass.: Harvard Business School Division of Research, 1971.

THOMPSON, GERALD E. *Statistics for Decisions: An Elementary Introduction.* Boston, Mass.: Little Brown & Company, 1972.

TRIBUS, MYRON. *Rational Descriptions, Decisions and Designs.* New York: Pergamon Press, 1969.

WASSON, CHESTER R. *Understanding Quantitative Analysis.* New York: Meredith Corporation, 1969.

WINKLER, R. L. *An Introduction to Bayesian Inference and Decision.* New York: Holt, Rinehart and Winston, Inc., 1972.

Index